The Bakke Case:
CHALLENGING AFFIRMATIVE ACTION

SUPREME COURT MILESTONES

The Bakke Case:
CHALLENGING
AFFIRMATIVE ACTION

REBECCA STEFOFF

 Marshall Cavendish
Benchmark

With special thanks to Professor David M. O'Brien of the Woodrow Wilson Department of Politics at the University of Virginia for reviewing the text of this book.

Marshall Cavendish Benchmark · 99 White Plains Road Tarrytown, NY 10591 · www.marshallcavendish.com · Copyright © 2006 by Rebecca Stefoff · All rights reserved. No part of this book may be reproduced or utilized in any form or by any means electronic or mechanical including photocopying, recording, or by any information storage and retrieval system, without permission from the copyright holders.

All Internet sites were available and the addresses were accurate when sent to press.

Library of Congress Cataloging-in-Publication Data

Stefoff, Rebecca, 1951– · The Bakke case : challenge to affirmative action / by Rebecca Stefoff.— · 1st ed. · p. cm. — (Supreme court milestones) · Includes bibliographical references and index. · Summary: "Describes the historical context of the case, *University of California Regents* v. *Bakke*, and details the claims made by both sides as well as the outcome, including excerpts from the Supreme Court justices decisions"— Provided by the publisher. · ISBN 0-7614-1939-X · 1. Bakke, Allan Paul—Trials, litigation, etc. 2. University of California (System). Regents—Trials, litigation, etc. 3. Discrimination in medical education—Law and legislation—United States. 4. Affirmative action programs—Law and legislation—United States. 5. Medical colleges— California—Admission. I. Title. II. Series. · KF228.B34S74 2005 · 344.73'0798—dc22 2004023444

Photo Research by Candlepants Incorporated

Cover Photo: Reuters/Corbis

The photographs in this book are used by permission and through the courtesy of: *Corbis*: 23, 24, 26, 29, 33, 92; Reuters, 1, 2-3, 109, 120, 122; Bettmann, 6, 10, 35, 65, 67, 108; *University of Washington, Special Collections*: (#uw23845z) 42, (#uw23844z) 46. *United States Supreme Court*: Vic Boswell/National Geographic Society, 51; Joe Lavenburg, National Geographic Society, 97; Simmie L. Knox, National Geographic Society; 104; Hugh Talman, Smithsonian Institute, 110; Dane Penlane, Smithsonian Institute, 124; *California State Archives*: 81; *Jason Doiy/The Recorder*: 83; AP/Wide World Photo/Walt Zeboski: 107.

Series design by Sonia Chaghatzbanian
Printed in China · 1 3 5 6 4 2

contents

A CROWD WAITS OUTSIDE THE U.S. SUPREME COURT, HOPING TO HEAR THE ARGUMENTS IN THE *BAKKE CASE*, IN WHICH ALLAN BAKKE CLAIMED THAT THE UNIVERSITY OF CALIFORNIA'S ADMISSIONS POLICIES DISCRIMINATED AGAINST HIM BECAUSE HE WAS WHITE.

one
"REVERSE DISCRIMINATION"

THe impressive stone BUILDING that houses the
United States Supreme Court stands in the heart of
Washington, D.C., across a broad street from the Capitol
building, where legislators make the laws that the justices
of the Court interpret and apply. Depending upon the business of the Supreme Court on any given day, members of
the public may enter the courtroom to watch and listen
as the justices hear arguments in a case. A typical audience
contains school groups on field trips, a sprinkling of law
students, a few members of the government or guests of the
justices, and some tourists exploring the nation's capital.

People do not usually get very excited about these
courtroom sessions, even though the Supreme Court is
the highest court in the land, even though its decisions
have occasionally reshaped American law and society.
The courtroom has four hundred seats for visitors.
Often, some of them remain empty. But on October 11,
1977, people clamored for seats.

As afternoon faded into evening, people lined up
outside the building, hoping to get a seat in the courtroom—not for that day, but for the next day. Three hundred seats had already been reserved for officials,
guests of the justices, and people who were involved in
the case that would be heard the following day, or who

had a special interest in it. Of the steadily growing crowd outside the Supreme Court building, only a hundred would get seats when the courtroom opened. Another hundred and fifty or so would be admitted in groups of ten to observe for three minutes during the Court session. Still, quite a few of those who waited through the October night would never make it into the courtroom.

On the following morning, some of the people who showed up outside the Supreme Court knew that they wouldn't get seats. They came not to observe but to make statements of their own. These demonstrators milled around in front of the Supreme Court building and on the opposite side of the street, holding signs and shouting slogans. Many of them were African Americans.

Security at the Court entrance was unusually tight on October 12. While people filed through the doors, guards carefully checked overcoat pockets and women's purses. Inside the courtroom, stewards set up extra chairs for the more than ninety newspaper and television journalists who showed up to observe and report on the day's arguments. Like the crowd waiting outside and the spectators taking their seats, the men and women of the press knew that history could be made that day. The Supreme Court was set to hear the difficult and controversial case known as *University of California Regents* v. *Bakke*. The outcome could profoundly affect the future of blacks and other minorities in America's schools, workplaces, and professions. Millions of people were passionately interested in the *Bakke* case because it opened a new chapter in the long, troubled saga of race relations in the United States.

"I want to study medicine"

At the heart of the case was a thirty-seven-year-old man named Allan Paul Bakke, who wanted to become a doctor. He had applied to the medical school of the University of California at Davis (UCDMS) and been rejected. Bakke was convinced that he had been denied the opportunity to go to medical school because UCDMS gave 16 percent of the places in each entering class to minority applicants. Bakke, who was white, claimed that he had been discriminated against because of his race. In a series of lawsuits that had finally risen to the Supreme Court, he argued that UCDMS had violated his civil rights.

Allan Bakke did not set out primarily to stir up a storm of controversy over race. On August 7, 1974, when he was starting to think about bringing a lawsuit against the University of California or another university that had also rejected his application to medical school, he wrote in a letter to a UCDMS official: "[M]y first concern is to be allowed to study medicine," adding that "challenging the concept of racial quotas is secondary." Still, Bakke knew that such a lawsuit would have effects far beyond his own education and career. It would become an attack on programs that some people thought were unfair, even illegal—programs that set aside quotas, or specific numbers or percentages, of admissions, jobs, or promotions for minority candidates who might be less well qualified than whites who sought the same opportunities. But while the trial dragged on for several years, Bakke stayed focused on the goal he had underlined in his second application to

REPORTERS AND PHOTOGRAPHERS CROWD AROUND ALLAN BAKKE AFTER HIS
FIRST DAY OF MEDICAL SCHOOL IN 1978. HE WAS NOT JUST ANY STUDENT—HE
WAS ATTENDING CLASSES BECAUSE THE U.S. SUPREME COURT RULING IN AN
HISTORIC AFFIRMATIVE ACTION CASE HAD FORCED THE SCHOOL TO ADMIT HIM.

UCDMS: "More than anything else in the world, *I want to study medicine*."

Race was not the only thing that affected Allan Bakke's application to medical school. Age was also a problem. When Bakke began asking medical schools about their requirements, he was more than thirty years old—above the age limit for admission to some schools. By the time he first applied to UCDMS, he was thirty-two.

Before the Age Discrimination Act of 1975 became law in 1979, medical schools openly favored younger applicants over older ones. The schools view their goal as providing society with medical practitioners. In theory, a younger graduate of medical school will practice medicine for more years before retiring than an older one will. For that reason, during the early 1970s medical schools regarded a younger candidate as a better investment of time and effort, if other factors were equal. Allan Bakke, however, did not let his age discourage him from pursuing his goal. He was determined to become a physician in spite of the fact that he had gotten a late start. If he succeeded, medicine would be his second professional education and his second career.

Bakke was born on February 4, 1940, in Minneapolis, Minnesota, although his family soon moved to Coral Gables, Florida, where Allan grew up. The family was solidly middle class: Allan's father was a mail carrier, his mother a schoolteacher. It was also solidly white—specifically, Scandinavian American. Like many Minnesotans, Bakke's parents were of Norwegian ancestry, and he inherited their fair hair, light skin, and blue eyes.

When it was time for college, Bakke returned to his birth state, Minnesota. He graduated from the University of Minnesota with a bachelor of science degree in mechanical engineering in 1962. He had earned a grade point average (GPA) of 3.51, out of a possible 4.0, and was elected to Pi Tau Sigma, the national honor society of mechanical engineers. After graduating, Bakke completed a year of graduate study in engineering.

To finance his university studies, Bakke had joined the Naval Reserve Officers Training Organization (ROTC), which paid his tuition and living expenses. In return, Bakke owed four years of military service. Although people in the reserves do not always have to perform military service, during the 1960s the United States became embroiled in the Vietnam War, and Allan Bakke was one of thousands of Americans who served in Southeast Asia. In September 1963 he entered the Marine Corps as a second lieutenant to fulfill his ROTC debt. Bakke spent seven months in Vietnam, commanding an antiaircraft missile unit in combat, and was promoted to captain. When he left the Marine Corps in September 1967, he qualified for veterans' benefits to help him continue his education. Bakke would be eligible for those benefits through the fall of 1976.

As soon as he left the Marine Corps, Bakke went to work at the Ames Research Center near San Francisco, California. A branch of the National Aeronautics and Space Administration (NASA), Ames was devoted to the design and testing of new, experimental aircraft and spacecraft. Bakke became assistant chief of the facility's equipment engineering branch. He also continued his graduate education at Stanford University in nearby Palo Alto. Stanford granted him a master's degree in mechanical engineering in June 1970.

Even before leaving Vietnam, however, Bakke had become interested in medicine and was thinking about going to medical school. By 1971, that interest had grown into a firm ambition. While working full time at Ames, Bakke went back to school again, enrolling in night classes at Stanford and San Jose State University. This time, he wasn't studying engineering. His new classes were in chemistry and biology—all of the courses required for applicants to medical school. Bakke also gained some real-life exposure to the medical profession by serving as a volunteer in the emergency room at El Camino Hospital in the town of Mountain View.

Bakke's Quest to Get In

The would-be medical student confronted the age issue head-on. In September 1971, Bakke wrote to several medical schools, including UCDMS, saying, "I am 31 years old, and my purpose in writing this letter is to determine whether my application would receive your consideration. I wish to avoid the wasted effort of applying to medical schools whose policy is automatic rejection of applicants my age." The answer he received from UCDMS, written by an associate dean of the school, was not encouraging, but it didn't completely close the door. The dean said that although UCDMS did not have a fixed age limit, "when an applicant is over thirty, his age is a serious factor which must be considered. . . . The Committee feels that an older applicant must be unusually highly qualified if he is to be seriously considered for one of the limited number of places in the entering class."

Bakke took the Medical College Admission Test (MCAT), required of everyone who intends to apply to medical school, and then sent applications to Northwestern University and the University of Southern California for the year 1972–1973. Both rejected him. He did not give up. For the 1973–1974 year, he applied to eleven schools, including UCDMS. In his straightforward style, he raised the issue of age in his applications, explaining that he had spent time in the military. "Four years was a high price to pay for my undergraduate education," he wrote in his application to UCDMS, "and I would hope that the admissions committee will not hold these years of service to America against me."

Four of the schools, including UCDMS, interviewed Bakke. At UCDMS, Bakke's interviewer was a professor of medical education, who summed up his impressions of Bakke in his report to the admissions committee:

On the grounds of motivation, academic record, potential promise, endorsement by persons capable of reasonable judgments, personal appearance and demeanor, maturity and probable contribution to balance in the class I believe that Mr. Bakke must be considered as a very desirable applicant to this medical school and I shall so recommend him.

But UCDMS, and the other ten schools as well, rejected Bakke's application. UCDMS, like other medical schools, gave each candidate a numerical score based on the candidate's GPA, MCAT scores, letters of recommendation, interview, and extracurricular activities or other experiences that would enrich the candidate's performance as student and physician. At the time of Bakke's first application to UCDMS, the maximum possible score for an applicant was 500. To be admitted, an applicant had to score at least 470. Bakke scored 468. Here, however, two other factors came into play.

One factor was timing. Because Bakke and his wife had spent several months in Iowa caring for her mother, who had lung cancer, Bakke was late in applying for the 1973–1974 school year. By the time he filed his application, many of the places in the 1973 entering class had already been filled. Some of those places had been filled by candidates whose scores were slightly lower than 470. However, with fewer seats available for the later applicants, the admissions committee became stricter about the score. It is possible that, if Bakke had applied earlier, his score would have been high enough to win him entry to UCDMS.

The second factor working against Bakke was the UCDMS admissions process, which eventually became the focus of the *Bakke* case. The medical school admitted one hundred candidates each year, but not all of them met the same standards. In fact, UCDMS had two admissions processes: regular and special.

UCDMS sorted applications for the 1973–1974 year into two groups based on Line 22 of the application form, which read: "Applicants from economically and educationally disadvantaged backgrounds are evaluated by a special subcommittee of the admissions committee. If you wish your application to be considered by this group, check this space." If an applicant checked that space, his or her application was reviewed, not by the regular admissions committee, but by the special subcommittee, also called the task force. The task force had been created in 1968 to increase the diversity of the medical school's students and faculty. At the time of Bakke's application, it consisted of five faculty members and eleven medical students. Three of the faculty members were white, two Asian American. All of the students were minorities.

The entering class had one hundred places. The task force was given sixteen of these slots to fill. And while the regular admissions committee automatically rejected any applicant whose GPA was lower than 2.5, the task force considered applicants with lower GPAs and lower MCAT scores. For the 1973–1974 year, the students admitted by the task force had an average GPA of 2.88 and an average score in the 35th percentile of the science section of the MCAT. The regular-admissions students had an average GPA of 3.49 and scored in the 85th percentile of the science MCAT.

Bakke was unhappy with UCDMS's rejection. In May 1973 he wrote to Dr. George Lowrey, the head of admissions to the medical school, saying, "I'm not yet willing to give up my commitment to become a physician." He received no reply, so he wrote again. This time he raised the issue that would make *Bakke* a Supreme Court case of national importance—the issue of race. Bakke wrote:

I feel compelled to pursue a further course of action. . . . Applicants chosen to be our doctors should be those presenting the best qualifications, both academic and personal . . . but I am convinced that a significant fraction of every current medical class is judged by a separate criterion. I am refer-

ring to quotas, open or covert, for racial minorities. Medicine needs the ablest and most dedicated
men in order to meet future health care needs. I
realize that the rationale for these quotas is that
they attempt to atone for past racial discrimination. But instituting a new racial bias, in favor of
minorities, is not a just solution. In fact, I believe
that admissions quotas based on race are illegal.
For this reason I am inquiring of friends . . . about
the possibility of formally challenging these
quotas through the courts. My main reason for
undertaking such action would be to secure
admission for myself—I consider that goal worth
fighting for in every legal or ethical way.

In that letter of July 1, 1973, Allan Bakke first mentioned the possibility of a lawsuit over racial preferences. More than four years later, in October 1977, the
Supreme Court was about to hear the arguments in that
lawsuit. The principal parties in the case were Allan
Bakke and the regents, or presiding officials, of the
University of California at Davis, but the case extended
far beyond those parties. The future of affirmative
action was at stake.

AFFirmative Action on Trial

The *Bakke* case was a direct challenge to affirmative
action, a policy of racial preferences that developed
during the late 1960s and 1970s. Affirmative action
called for schools, employers, and other institutions to
take active steps to admit, hire, promote, and advance
minorities through programs like the special admissions
program at UCDMS. But in the eyes of some, including

Allan Bakke, affirmative action was just a new form of racial discrimination, and racial discrimination had been made illegal by the Civil Rights Act of 1964. Bakke knew that some of the minority students who had been admitted under UCDMS's special admissions program had test scores and grade point averages lower than his own. Less-qualified minority students, in other words, had been favored over a better-qualified white student. Bakke believed he had been denied entrance to medical school because he was white.

Bakke's complaint and others like it introduced a new phrase into America's conversations about racial matters: "reverse discrimination." It referred to injuries that white people believed they had suffered as a result of favoritism shown to blacks and other minorities—groups that had formerly been victims of racial discrimination themselves. The phrase summed up the anxiety and unease that some white people felt as race relations in America changed during the 1970s. Equally anxious and uneasy, however, were African Americans and other minorities. To many people of color, affirmative action was no more than society owed them after generations of discrimination and oppression. To some of them, it was a vital link to a better life.

Bakke was about much more than one man's desire to go to medical school, or his right to do so. The case forced the nine Supreme Court justices to reexamine the Civil Rights Act of 1964 and the U.S. Constitution. In the end, it brought deep disagreements among the justices and a painful and impassioned reinterpretation of the motto that is carved in stone above the main doorway of the Supreme Court building: "Equal Justice Under Law."

WHO'S a minority now?

Affirmative action was meant to give certain groups of people a boost in education, in the workplace, and in American society in general. Those groups were "minorities," a term that people on both sides of the affirmative action issue have used for decades. But just who is a minority?

In July 1963, after President John F. Kennedy declared the need for a new civil rights act for the nation, the U.S. House of Representatives held hearings on some of the issues that such an act might raise. During the hearings, Congressman Peter Rodino of New Jersey asked James Farmer, a spokesperson for the Congress of Racial Equality (CORE), how CORE felt about racial quotas in jobs and schools. "We are not one of the organizations that believe in a quota," Farmer replied. "We do believe, however, in aggressive action to secure the employment of minorities, but not in terms of a quota." Everyone present knew what Farmer meant by "minorities." The rest of his exchange with Rodino made clear that he was talking in particular about African Americans, or "Negroes," the correct term for blacks at the time.

The term "minorities" has included many other groups identified by their race, ethnicity, national origin, or religion: Asian Americans, Native Americans, Hispanics, Jews, Catholics, and more. Separately and together, such groups have been in the minority within the total population of the United States, where the majority of people are whites of European Christian descent. In strictly numerical terms, a majority is more than half of a total, and a minority is less than half. But what happens if the balance shifts, and the minorities become the majority?

The balance has already shifted in some places.

Certain urban centers have long had black or Hispanic populations that outnumber their white residents. And by 2000, whites had become a minority in the states of California, Hawaii, and New Mexico, as well as the District of Columbia. Within less than half a century, the same will be true for the United States as a whole.

The primary source of information about the racial and ethnic makeup of the American population is the U.S. Census, conducted every ten years. Census data shows changes in the majority-minority balance since the time of the *Bakke* case, which took place between the 1970 and 1980 censuses. In 1970, 87.5 percent of Americans were white, 11.1 percent were black, and 1.4 percent identified themselves as belonging to another race. Ten years later, not long after the end of *Bakke*, the white majority had dropped to 83.1 percent. The percentage of blacks had risen a bit, to 11.7 percent. The biggest growth was in the category of other races, which had risen to 5.2 percent of the total. By 2000, the U.S. population had changed even more dramatically: 75.1 of the total population was white, 12.3 percent was black, and 12.5 percent belonged to some other category. During *Bakke*, America was much more than four-fifths white. At the dawn of the twenty-first century, it was barely three-quarters white.

Census data does more than provide a snapshot of the current population. It is the raw material for demographics, the study of population features and trends. Census data gives a forecast of where the nation is headed—and it appears to be headed toward a much more multiracial, multicultural population. In 2004, demographers for the U.S. Census Bureau released a projection for the future, based on existing trends. If their projection holds true, by 2050 the population of the

United States will be 50.1 percent white—just a shade more than half. And at some point soon afterward, the balance will shift, and white Americans will become a racial minority. What will that mean for such concepts as racial justice and affirmative action? Will we redefine "minority"? Or, as Justice Harry A. Blackmun hoped when he wrote his opinion in the *Bakke* case, will American society "reach a stage of maturity where [affirmative] action along this line is no longer necessary"?

TWO
RIGHTING A WRONG OR STACKING THE DECK?

For several hundred years, racial inequality was law in America. The law changed, but slowly. People's attitudes and behavior changed even more slowly. The *Bakke* case unfolded against a background of other battles over racial justice—battles fought on slave plantations and in city streets as well as in Congress and in courtrooms.

Race relations in America began, tragically, with slavery. Africans were present in the British North American colonies from the start, and by the middle of the seventeenth century, some colonies had laws that defined racial categories. In 1661, for example, Virginia passed a law that recognized the existence and limits of slavery. Under this law, whites could not be enslaved, although they could be bound into certain types of enforced servitude, but blacks and Native Americans could be slaves. Laws also spelled out slaves' legal status, which was not much different from other forms of property. Driving this system of racial discrimination was the continual need for more workers, especially in the Southern colonies. The Southern economy was based on plantation crops, such as tobacco and cotton, that required much labor.

Not all colonists supported slavery. During the eigh-

THE ECONOMY OF THE AMERICAN SOUTH WAS BASED ON CASH CROPS SUCH AS COTTON, TOBACCO, AND RICE, WHICH WERE GROWN ON LARGE PLANTATIONS WITH A HIGH DEMAND FOR LABOR. FROM THE EARLIEST DAYS OF THE AMERICAN COLONIES TO THE CIVIL WAR, PLANTATION OWNERS SOUGHT TO MEET THEIR LABOR NEEDS THROUGH SLAVERY.

teenth century, the abolition movement, dedicated to ending slavery, arose in both England and the Northern colonies in North America. After the American Revolution established the United States as an independent nation, the Northern states outlawed slavery. Even in the South, some slave owners freed their slaves. Yet many African Americans remained enslaved in the Southern states, fueling abolitionists' fervor. Tensions over slavery rose as the nation expanded westward and settlers colonized new frontier territories. Each territory was destined to become one or more states, and for each new state Congress had to

IN THE 1857 CASE OF *SCOTT V. SANDFORD*, SOMETIMES CALLED THE *DRED SCOTT* CASE, THE SUPREME COURT DEFINED AFRICAN AMERICANS AS PROPERTY— A DECISION THAT LATER LAWS, RULINGS, AND CONSTITUTIONAL AMENDMENTS HAVE REVERSED.

decide whether it would be a slave state or a free state, try-ing to preserve a national balance between the two. Furious conflicts erupted over the issue. So violent was the fighting in one frontier territory that the place was called "Bleeding Kansas."

CIVIL war and Reconstruction

By the middle of the nineteenth century, the nation was headed toward the Civil War, which would pit North against South and forever change the status of African Americans. In 1857, the U.S. Supreme Court's decision in the *Scott* v. *Sandford* case infuriated abolitionists and helped draw the battle lines in the coming conflict.

Dred Scott was an African American who, with the help of abolitionist lawyers, sued for freedom from his owner. Scott's claim for freedom was based on the fact that although he had been purchased as a slave in the slave state of Missouri, he had lived with his owner for a time in the free state of Illinois and the free territory of Wisconsin. This, argued Scott and his lawyers, made him free. The high court disagreed. It ruled that Scott was still a slave. Because he was a slave, he could not be a citizen, and because he was not a citizen, he could not bring a lawsuit against his owner. Chief Justice Roger Taney went further, declaring in his decision that African Americans "are not included, and were not intended to be included, under the word 'citizens' in the Constitution" and that black people "had no rights which the white man was bound to respect." In the *Dred Scott* case, the highest court in the land confirmed the view that African Americans were property, not people.

Four years later, the Civil War began. With it came the transformation of African Americans' legal status.

FREDERICK DOUGLASS, SHOWN AT THE CENTER OF A CONSTELLATION OF AFRICAN AMERICANS IN THIS NINETEENTH-CENTURY ILLUSTRATION, WAS A PASSIONATE SPOKESPERSON FOR ABOLITION AND ONE OF THE LEADING FORCES OF THE ANTISLAVERY MOVEMENT IN THE UNITED STATES.

President Abraham Lincoln's Emancipation Proclamation of 1863 freed enslaved African Americans in areas held by the Confederacy, the rebellious Southern states. After the war ended in 1865, the Thirteenth Amendment to the Constitution formally abolished slavery in all parts of the United States, including the former Confederacy. The end of legal enslavement, however, was only the beginning of a new kind of oppression for many freed blacks.

Southern property owners and lawmakers responded to the Thirteenth Amendment by passing new laws called Black Codes. Although blacks were now citizens under the Constitution, the Black Codes created a separate category of citizenship for them, one that denied them the rights and privileges of other citizens, such as voting or serving on juries. The Black Codes created a system of segregation in which African Americans could be banned from "white-only" restaurants, hotels, and train cars. The Codes also limited blacks' opportunities to own land, obtain education, and fill jobs.

Help came from the North—for a while. The United States Congress was dominated by a group of powerful, mostly Northern lawmakers called the Radical Republicans. Former abolitionists who now supported equality for African Americans, the Radical Republicans forced Congress to pass civil rights laws. In 1868 Congress added the Fourteenth Amendment to the Constitution. It granted full citizenship to all persons born in the United States and also required the states to give *all* citizens "equal protection" and "due process" of law.

The Fifteenth Amendment, added in 1870, guaranteed every male adult citizen the right to vote "regardless of race, color, creed, national origin, or previous condition of servitude."

The Radical Republicans also oversaw the start of Reconstruction, as the postwar reorganizing and rebuilding of the South was called. In addition to stationing troops throughout the South to enforce the law and protect blacks, the federal government set up educational and economic programs to help the former slaves. More than a century later, when delivering his opinion in the *Bakke* case, Supreme Court Justice Thurgood Marshall likened those programs to the affirmative action programs that *Bakke* challenged. "After the Civil War," Marshall reminded the nation, "our Government started several 'affirmative action programs.'"

That first experiment with affirmative action produced some dramatic results. In 1867, the ten states of the former Confederacy had more registered black voters than white ones. African Americans were elected to the House of Representatives and the Senate. Black Americans appeared to be on their way to citizenship in the full sense of the word—but that prospect frightened and angered many people in the South, and some in the North. Before long, a backlash against black equality was under way. White terror groups such as the Ku Klux Klan used threats and violence to keep blacks from voting and claiming other rights of citizenship. The Radical Republicans lost control of Congress and also abandoned their commitment to racial equality. In

RACIAL PREJUDICE WAS FATAL FOR THOUSANDS OF AFRICAN AMERICANS WHO WERE MURDERED, OFTEN PUBLICLY LYNCHED BY MOBS, IN THE NINETEENTH AND TWENTIETH CENTURIES.

1877, President Rutherford B. Hayes, a Republican, withdrew federal troops from the South, and the era of Reconstruction ended.

racism and the supreme court

After Reconstruction, several major Supreme Court decisions reversed much of the progress that had been made toward racial equality and civil rights for all. In 1883, the Court overturned the Civil Rights Act of 1875, which had made it illegal for nongovernmental entities to discriminate by race. The Court's 1883 ruling meant that railroad companies, restaurants, hotels, and other privately owned and operated businesses could provide services to whites and not to blacks, or could provide different classes of service according to race.

As a result of this decision, state and local legislatures in Southern and border states felt free to pass new laws that limited African Americans' freedoms. These Jim Crow laws, as they were called, created a system of organized, institutionalized segregation, or separation by race. Blacks had to ride in the backs of streetcars—if they were permitted to board them at all. They could not use schools, textbooks, water fountains, ticket lines, libraries, beaches, or hundreds of other facilities that were set aside for the use of whites only. In the courtrooms of Atlanta, Georgia, black witnesses could not swear to tell the truth, the whole truth, and nothing but the truth on the same Bible that white witnesses used. In Kentucky, black and white citizens lived by law on opposite sides of the street.

An African American named Homer Plessy challenged Jim Crow laws and segregation in a case that reached the Supreme Court in 1896. *Plessy* v. *Ferguson* concerned a Louisiana law that prevented a passenger on a train from entering "a coach or compartment to which by race he does not belong." Plessy argued that the law violated the Fourteenth Amendment by denying him equal justice and due process of law. The Court's ruling was a victory for segregation. By an eight to one majority, the Court held that the principle of equal rights did not require a forced mingling of different races. "If one race be inferior to the other socially," ran the decision, "the Constitution of the United States cannot put them on the same plane." The Court held that laws could not abolish "social instincts" or "distinctions based upon physical differences," and that separate facilities for blacks and whites were legal as long as they were equal. This concept of "separate but equal" would remain in force as the legal basis of segregation for another half century.

One Supreme Court justice dissented, or disagreed, with the majority opinion in *Plessy* v. *Ferguson.* In his dissenting opinion, Justice John Marshall Harlan wrote, "Our Constitution is color-blind, and neither knows nor tolerates classes among citizens. In respect to civil rights, all citizens are equal before the law." Harlan was opposed to segregation and supported racial equality. Decades later, during *Bakke,* his concept of a "color-blind" Constitution would be adopted by people opposed to affirmative action.

THE CHANGING PICTURE OF CIVIL RIGHTS

In the early twentieth century, racial equality appeared farther away than it had been since the days of slavery. The *Plessy* decision had spawned new Jim Crow laws and stricter enforcement of the old ones. Intolerance and prejudice seemed as strong as ever. After President Theodore Roosevelt, elected in 1901, invited African-American leader Booker T. Washington to dinner at the White House, a Memphis, Tennessee, newspaper called the president's action "the most damnable outrage ever perpetrated by any citizen of the United States." Prejudice took far uglier forms as well: Thousands of African Americans were brutally lynched—murdered by mob violence—most of them in the South.

But at the same time, civil rights activists, both black and white, were struggling to promote social and racial justice. In 1909 they formed the National Association for the Advancement of Colored People (NAACP), still one of the most important and influential civil rights organizations. One step at a time, the nation's lawmakers and courts, and the general public, inched closer to tolerance. Some key steps involved equal access to education for blacks and whites. The case of *Sweatt* v. *Painter*, for example, involved a black man named Herman Marion Sweatt who wanted to attend the University of Texas law school. A state law banned African Americans from entering the school. Sweatt sued the university, which lost the case and grudgingly admitted him—then created a separate "law school" for him to attend alone. This facility consisted of rented rooms in which two lawyers taught the

EQUALITY

In 1901, President Theodore Roosevelt's invitation to African-American leader Booker T. Washington to dine at the White House caused one Southern paper to rave that the president had committed the worst "outrage" by any American citizen, ever.

African-American student. Sweatt claimed that this separate facility was inferior to the main law school. The case went to the Supreme Court, which ruled on it in 1950. The Court's decision was that the ability to interact and debate with other students was a key part of a law student's education, and that the University of Texas could not legally deprive Sweatt of it. The Court ordered the law school to admit Sweatt to the general student population.

Sweatt v. *Painter* struck a blow against segregated education but did not abolish it. That decision came four years later, in one of the most significant cases in Supreme Court history: *Brown* v. *Board of Education*. A cluster of five cases that challenged segregation in public schools, *Brown* v. *Board of Education* was argued before the Supreme Court by Thurgood Marshall, then legal director of the NAACP. In a unanimous decision, the Court ruled, "We conclude that in the field of public education the doctrine of 'separate but equal' has no place." With this ruling, the Supreme Court overturned the *Plessy* decision. It ordered segregated school systems to integrate white and black students in the same schools "with all deliberate speed."

"All deliberate speed," however, is a vague phrase, lacking in specific details such as timetables or methods. Although *Brown* was an enormous victory for civil rights, it did not integrate the nation's schools overnight. In some places, desegregation took years, or even decades, and involved a lot of conflict. Nor did *Brown* v. *Board of Education* address segregation in settings other than public education. But in the years that followed, other cases tackled the issue of segregation, which gradually began to disappear from American life.

Erasing segregation took more—much more—than legal rulings. Getting those rulings enforced, ending segregation in reality instead of merely in words, required a long and vigorous movement of political protest. Led by civil rights groups such as the NAACP and the Southern Christian Leadership Conference (SCLC), supported by white as well as black activists from all over the country, the movement concentrated its

YEARS BEFORE THE *BAKKE* CASE, TEXAS MAIL CARRIER HERMAN SWEATT SUED
THE UNIVERSITY OF TEXAS LAW SCHOOL FOR DISCRIMINATING AGAINST HIM ON
RACIAL GROUNDS. HE WON THE CASE IN THE U.S. SUPREME COURT, FORCING
THE SCHOOL TO INTEGRATE. SWEATT'S ATTORNEY WAS THURGOOD MARSHALL,
WHO WOULD BE A MEMBER OF THE COURT WHEN BAKKE BROUGHT HIS CASE.

efforts in Southern states where segregation was most deeply rooted. Activists organized voter registration drives, conducted sit-ins and boycotts, and marched in the streets. Some were arrested or beaten, or both. A few were killed.

The momentum of the civil rights movement, though, could not be stopped. It generated new laws that, together with *Brown* and other court cases, redrew the picture of civil rights in the United States. The most important of these laws was the Civil Rights Act of 1964. This federal law banned discrimination by race, color, religion, or national origin (the act was later amended to include gender) in public places, government-supported agencies, and federally funded programs. The act also required the desegregation of public facilities and outlawed discrimination in many kinds of employment. The following year, Congress passed the Voting Rights Act, which specifically banned racial discrimination by state governments in voter registration and in conducting elections. Later laws and court decisions began the process of dismantling certain forms of discrimination by private individuals, institutions, and groups.

EXECUTIVE ORDERS

Even before the Civil Rights Act of 1964, a new term had entered the national conversation about race. That term was affirmative action, and it came from Executive Order 10925, issued by President John F. Kennedy in 1961.

An executive order is a directive from the executive branch of government, represented by the president. Because executive orders are not passed by Congress, they are not federal laws; however, unless Congress overrules them, they have the effect of law. Before Kennedy, Presidents Franklin D. Roosevelt and Harry S. Truman had used executive orders to ban racial discrimination by the federal government and in the military. Kennedy, with Executive Order 10925, established the President's Committee on Equal Employment Opportunity. The Committee's task was to end discrimination not just by the federal government but also by all of its contractors—that is, by everyone doing business with the federal government. A few years later, Title VII of the Civil Rights Act of 1964 established the Equal Employment Opportunity Commission as a permanent federal body.

Executive Order 10925 required government contractors to "take affirmative action, to ensure that applicants are employed, and that employees are treated during their employment, without regard to their race, creed, color, or national origin." The order banned discrimination but said nothing about special efforts to advance minorities. Later executive orders, however, extended the scope of 10925. Executive Order 11246, issued in 1965 and amended two years later, required federal agencies to "establish and maintain a positive program of equal employment opportunity." Agencies could use "numerical goals and timetables" in fulfilling this mission. A related 1970 order from the Department of Labor required each government contractor to develop "an acceptable affirmative action program" focused on the hiring and fair treatment of "Negroes, American Indians, Orientals, and Spanish Surnamed Americans"—or, as it would be expressed today, African Americans, Native Americans, Asian Americans, and Hispanic Americans. Again, women were added in a later amendment.

In introducing affirmative action, the federal government wanted to do more than just end discrimination against minorities and women. Affirmative action was intended to go beyond giving everyone a "level playing field." It was supposed to be a remedy for past discrimination, an attempt to counteract the effects of racial inequality. President Lyndon B. Johnson expressed this goal in a 1965 speech to the graduating class of Howard University, a historically black college:

[F]reedom is not enough. You do not wipe away the scars of centuries by saying, Now, you are free to go where you want, do as you desire, and choose the leaders you please. You do not take a man who for years has been hobbled by chains, liberate him, bring him to the starting line of a race, saying, "You are free to compete with all the others," and still justly believe you have been completely fair. Thus it is not enough to open the gates of opportunity. All our citizens must have the ability to walk through those gates. This is the next and most profound stage of the battle for civil rights. We seek not just freedom but opportunity—not just legal equity but human ability—not just equality as a right and a theory, but equality as a fact and a result.

For and Against Affirmative Action

Throughout the 1960s and 1970s, affirmative action programs appeared in various settings. Public institutions, government agencies, and federal contractors were the most visible of these settings, but some private schools, companies, and organizations also took definite steps to attract, welcome, and include minorities. By promoting affirmative action in employment and education, a series of presidents moved national and state policy beyond the "color-blind" Constitution of Justice Harlan. Instead of the strict equality that some legal historians have called race-neutral, affirmative action gave preference, or favorable treatment, to members of some racial groups.

Many colleges and universities—the institutions that would be examined in the *Bakke* case—came to see racial, ethnic, and cultural diversity of both students and faculty as a desirable goal. Affirmative action was a tool for creating diversity on campuses, or for increasing it where it already existed to some degree. Colleges and universities took various approaches to affirmative action, but their programs and policies fell into three general categories.

One category consisted of programs formed specifically to seek out well-qualified minority applicants. Such programs consider race along with other factors when deciding which candidates to admit. This kind of program, sometimes called the Harvard model because it has been used at Harvard University, actively works to increase diversity on campus but does not apply numerical goals. A second type of program does create numerical goals for minority students but requires those students to meet other standards for admission, such as test scores. If a school using this type of affirmative action program doesn't receive applications from enough qualified minority students in any given year, it will not meet its target number or percentage.

A third type of program, sometimes called a quota or set-aside program, also allots a specific number of places for minority students in each entering class, but always fills all of those places. To ensure that all set-aside places are filled, such programs typically use dual admissions processes, as UCDMS did in the *Bakke* case. They lower or relax the standards for minority applicants, which means that some minority students are admitted with lower test scores or grade averages than some white students who are rejected. Such programs give preferential treatment to minorities *because* they are minorities. Most of the controversy and strong feeling over affirmative action concerns preferential programs that use quotas or set-asides.

Supporters of affirmative action believed that it was the appropriate way to undo the lingering effects of discrimination. They saw affirmative action as correcting the injuries that had been done to racial minorities, especially to African Americans, who had inherited the legacy of legal enslavement. These defenders of affirmative action saw a color-blind, race-neutral world as the long-term ideal. To achieve that goal in the real world, however, it was necessary to offset years of mistreatment with a helping hand.

Opponents of affirmative action, on the other hand, regarded it as replacing one form of unfairness with another. If it was wrong to select people for ill treatment because of their race, it must be equally wrong to select them for positive treatment by race—or to penalize another group, white people, because of their race. Two wrongs, in the eyes of these critics, did not make a right. That belief strengthened during the late 1970s, when an economic downturn filled many Americans with concern for their own well-being. With a million college graduates unable to find the jobs for which they had trained, competition for advancement grew keener. If the pie were not big enough to give everyone a piece, some felt, then the pieces should be handed out impartially, based on individual merit and not on membership in a group. (In reality, college admissions may be influenced by factors other than either race or merit. Such factors include being the child of alumni and having influential family connections.)

Did affirmative action right an old injustice, or did it unfairly stack the deck on the basis of race? Supporters and opponents alike knew that the most pressing question about affirmative action was: Is it legal?

THREE
BEFORE *BAKKE*:
THE *DEFUNIS* CASE

THE LEGALITY OF AFFIRMATIVE ACTION in education would be tested through a challenge to the admissions program of a professional school at a university. For a few years in the early 1970s, it seemed as if Marco DeFunis's lawsuit against the University of Washington law school would settle the issue.

MARCO DEFUNIS JR., A WHITE JEWISH UNDERGRADUATE AT THE UNIVERSITY OF WASHINGTON, SUED THE UNIVERSITY FOR ADMISSION TO ITS LAW SCHOOL ON THE GROUNDS THAT HE HAD BEEN DISCRIMINATED AGAINST BECAUSE OF AFFIRMATIVE ACTION—AND WON.

Four years before *Bakke*, the U.S. Supreme Court heard the case of *DeFunis* v. *Odegaard*. It concerned the very same point of law that Allan Bakke's attorneys later raised in his case: Had a preferential admissions policy to promote affirmative action violated the civil rights of a rejected white applicant? The case stirred up a heated debate on both sides of the issue. It roused expectations that the Supreme Court would finally rule on the vexing question of affirmative action in higher education. If the Court had done so, the *Bakke* case might never have happened. Yet the Court avoided answering the questions raised by *DeFunis* for one simple reason: Marco DeFunis, unlike Allan Bakke, got what he wanted.

TWO Rejections

Getting into law school became much harder after the mid-1960s. The number of people hoping to become attorneys increased far more rapidly than the number of available places in law schools. Between the 1964–1965 school year and the 1975–1976 year, the number of first-year law students doubled. But during that same decade, the number of applications to law schools multiplied by about three and a half times, for a total of 134,000 applications in 1975. The result was a more competitive climate for college graduates seeking admission to law school.

Marco DeFunis Jr., a white, Jewish native of Washington State, went to college at the University of Washington in Seattle. He earned a GPA of 3.6 out of a possible 4.0; during his junior and senior years, his lowest grade was an A⁻. While attending college, DeFunis also worked part time for the Seattle Parks and Recreation Department and taught religious classes for children at his synagogue. He graduated in 1970 with high honors and a bachelor of arts degree in political science. All in all, he was an outstanding student and an excellent candidate for graduate school.

DeFunis, who wanted to become a lawyer, applied to a six law schools for the 1970–1971 year. He was one of about 70,000 students who applied to the country's law schools that year. There was room for half of them. DeFunis was luckier than many. He was accepted at the law schools of the state universities in the two neighboring states, Idaho and Oregon. In addition, two private law schools accepted his application. But the school he most wanted to attend, for financial reasons and to remain near his family, was the University of Washington law school (UWLS), which rejected him.

Rather than attend one of the other schools, DeFunis decided to wait a year, retake the Law School Aptitude Test (LSAT), and try again at UWLS. A new LSAT score of 668 placed DeFunis in the top 7 percent of applicants in the nation and was significantly higher than his previous score of 582. Armed with this impressive score, DeFunis applied again to UWLS for the 1971–1972 school year. A total of 1,601 students had applied for the 150 first-year places available at UWLS that year.

In July of 1971, DeFunis got his second letter of rejection from UWLS. Now DeFunis felt certain that he had been rejected because UWLS reserved places for minority candidates and evaluated those candidates by different standards than it used for white, mainstream candidates. Through a mutual acquaintance, the story of the young man's disappointment came to the ears of Josef Diamond, the senior partner in a Seattle law firm. Diamond, who was already concerned about the question of minority admissions at UWLS, decided to represent DeFunis. The lawyer first met with UWLS officials, hoping to persuade them to change their position on DeFunis's application. When that effort failed, Diamond took the matter to court. DeFunis filed a civil suit against UWLS, charging it with reverse discrimination. The suit named Charles Odegaard as defendant because he was president of the University of Washington. In his filing DeFunis claimed that the school had violated the civil rights that were guaranteed to him under the Fourteenth Amendment of the Constitution.

Law School Admissions on Trial

DeFunis v. *Odegaard* drew attention to the admissions policy of the law school at the University of Washington. Odegaard had led the move to craft that policy along the guidelines of affirmative action. Intended to increase UWLS's racial diversity, the policy was administered by a seven-person admissions committee made up of five professors or administrators and two students. Each incoming application was reviewed by one member of the committee, who then made a recommendation to the full committee, which made the final decision on each application.

Committee members evaluated the incoming applications in three ways. First, the committee member calculated each applicant's predicted first-year average (PFYA). This score was based on several numerical factors, including the applicant's LSAT score, his or her college GPA, the quality of the applicant's college, and the difficulty of his or her college courses. The maximum possible PFYA was 81. In addition, the committee member determined whether the applicant was likely to make "significant contributions to law school classrooms and the community at large" and also looked at the applicant's "social or ethnic background."

The PFYA was the first dividing line. Applicants with PFYAs of 77 or higher were admitted. Those with PFYAs of 74.5 or lower were rejected. Those whose scores fell between 74.5 and 77 would be reevaluated, possibly

PRESIDENT CHARLES ODEGAARD IS SURROUNDED BY COLLEAGUES AT THE UNIVERSITY OF WASHINGTON. THEY MADE THE DECISION NOT TO ADMIT MARCO DEFUNIS JR. ON THE GROUNDS OF AFFIRMATIVE ACTION, BUT WERE OVERRULED IN THE STATE SUPREME COURT CASE THAT FOLLOWED.

admitted, or placed on a waiting list. Two exceptions to these standards existed. Military veterans who had previously been admitted to UWLS but had been prevented from attending by military service were automatically admitted. And applicants from four particular minority groups were considered preferred candidates. Those groups were African American, Hispanic American, Native American, and Filipino American. Members of other minorities, such as Chinese Americans and Japanese Americans, became part of the general admissions pool, along with white applicants. The preferred minority candidates formed a separate, smaller pool.

Preferred candidates received two kinds of special screening. When possible, applications were matched by race with members of the admissions committee. An application from an African American, for example, went to a black committee member. Even more significantly, the admissions committee placed less importance on preferred candidates' PFYAs than on those of regular candidates, and they compared preferred candidates only with each other, not with the general applicant pool. This meant that minorities seeking to enter UWLS had to compete only with each other, not with all other applicants, and that they could be admitted with PFYAs lower than the 74.5 that was the minimum for the general pool.

The law school's stated goal for minority admissions was 15 to 20 percent of each entering class. This would translate to between 22 and 30 students in a first-year class of 150. However, although only 4 percent of all applications to enter UWLS in the fall of 1971 had come from minorities, 44 of the entering students, or almost 30 percent of them, were minorities. Many of them had scored below 74.5 on the PFYA. DeFunis's PFYA of 76.23 was higher than the PFYAs of 38 of the minority students who had been admitted. DeFunis had also scored higher than 22 veterans and 16 non-veteran, non-minority students who were admitted. Twenty-nine other white applicants with PFYAs higher than DeFunis's had also been rejected. DeFunis, however, was the one who sued.

THROUGH THE STATE COURTS

DeFunis v. *Odegaard* went to trial in Superior Court for King County, Washington, not long after DeFunis received his second rejection letter from UWLS. Both sides in the suit agreed that the affirmative action program at UWLS gave preferential treatment to minority candidates. The question was not whether such a program existed but whether it was constitutional.

Attorney Diamond, arguing on behalf of DeFunis, claimed that the Fourteenth Amendment, which guarantees all citizens equal protection and due process under law, prohibits any form of discrimination that groups people by race and treats them differently because of their race. It didn't matter that the goal was to help racial minorities, not to harm them— "positive" racism was still racism, with the result that white applicants like his client suffered discrimination.

Under the legal standard known as compelling interest, the state can limit or restrict rights in pursuit of an important, overriding goal. An institution that had deliberately and knowingly discriminated against minorities in the past, for example, might be able to prove that it had a compelling interest in using preferential programs temporarily, to right a specific wrong. But as Diamond pointed out, the UWLS was innocent of deliberate discrimination in the past. He argued that the school therefore had no compelling interest in letting racial quotas override DeFunis's right to equal protection.

Slade Gorton, the state attorney for Washington, presented UWLS's side of the case. Gorton claimed that UWLS and all law schools did have a compelling interest in using racial preferences to overcome the history of racial and ethnic discrimination that affected the entire nation. UWLS's preferential admissions policy *was* a form of discrimination, but it was benign, or positive, discrimination. Such policies would increase diversity on the nation's campuses, in its professional schools, and in its professions. Diversity on campus enhanced the educational experience for all. Diversity in law schools and in state bars would give minority communities a chance to achieve fair representation in one of the country's key professions. These were admirable, democratic goals and did not conflict with the Constitution.

Judge Lloyd Shorett decided the case in favor of DeFunis. "Public education must be equally available to all regardless of race," Shorett declared, quoting from the Supreme Court's landmark decision in *Brown* v. *Board of Education*. Adding that "the Fourteenth Amendment could no longer be stretched to accommodate the needs of any race," the judge concluded, "the only safe rule is to treat all races alike." Shorett ordered UWLS to admit DeFunis for the fall 1971 term, which was about to start. He also specified that his decision applied only to DeFunis, the plaintiff in the case, to prevent all of the other applicants who had been rejected from pressing their own claims.

The law school admitted DeFunis as ordered. At the same time, however, it appealed Shorett's decision to a higher court. Normally, an appeal from Superior Court would go to the Court of Appeals. But because the central element in *DeFunis* v. *Odegaard* was an interpretation of the Constitution, Gorton was able to skip one level in the appeals process. He took his appeal directly to the Washington State Supreme Court, which heard the arguments in the case in May 1972. Not until March 1973 did the state's highest court deliver its decision. By a vote of six to two, the court overturned Shorett's decision and ruled in favor of UWLS.

Two members of the court had agreed with Shorett's decision and Diamond's arguments in the lower court. "The circle of inequality," they wrote in their dissenting opinion, "cannot be broken by shifting the inequities from one man to his neighbor." The majority of the court, however, agreed with Gorton that the Fourteenth Amendment prohibited invidious, or harmful, discrimination. The Constitution, they ruled, would allow positive discrimination, such as preferential admissions, if the goal were "to promote integration and undo the effects of past discrimination." UWLS, in short, did have a compelling interest in maintaining racial quotas in admissions, even if this policy meant that some qualified white candidates might not get into the law school.

What did the new decision mean for Marco DeFunis, now more than halfway through the three-year UWLS program? He asked the state supreme court to rehear the case, but his request was denied. His position was awkward. On one hand, he had no great desire to continue a legal process that had made him unpopular with some of his fellow students. On the other hand, he wanted to finish his program at UWLS. Although the school had not asked him to leave, he knew that its administrators now had the legal right to remove him from the program at any time, if they chose.

Not wanting to risk dismissal, during the summer of 1973 DeFunis appealed the state supreme court's decision to the highest court in the land, the U.S. Supreme Court. The Court was in recess for the summer, so Associate Justice William O. Douglas of the Supreme Court, whose responsibilities included reviewing appeals from the state of Washington, issued a legal order known as a stay of action. This order suspended the state supreme court's ruling, or placed it on hold, until the U.S. Supreme Court

JUSTICE WILLIAM O. DOUGLAS ISSUED THE ORDER THAT ALLOWED MARCO DEFUNIS JR. TO ATTEND LAW SCHOOL WHILE HIS CASE WAS WAITING ITS TURN BEFORE THE SUPREME COURT.

could decide whether or not to hear the case. In effect, Shorett's original ruling remained in force. DeFunis could not be ejected from UWLS before the Supreme Court acted.

"DUCKING THE ISSUE"

A term of the U.S. Supreme Court begins on the first Monday of October and lasts until the following June or early July. During that period, the nine justices of the Court alternate between sittings, during which they hear arguments in the courtroom, and recesses, during which they study and discuss cases. The Court can hear only a small fraction of the more than 9,000 cases that are presented to it each term (the number of cases has increased dramatically, up from 2,313 in 1960, but the number of justices and the Court's general procedures have never changed). During the 1970s and 1980s, the Court granted plenary review to between 150 and 180 cases a year, which meant that attorneys could present oral arguments before the justices in these cases. Since that time, the number of cases granted review in a year has dropped to fewer than 100. The Court typically delivers formal written opinions on 80 to 90 of them.

The vast majority of cases heard before the Supreme Court are appealed to it from lower courts. Nearly all of them reach the Court in the form of requests for a writ, or order, of *certiorari*, a Latin legal term that refers to moving records of a case from a lower to a higher court. When deciding whether to grant certiorari to a particular case, the justices of the Supreme Court consider several points. Does the case involve major questions of law, especially interpreting the Constitution, that should be resolved for the public good? Have two lower federal courts, or a federal and a state court, delivered conflicting

THROUGH THE COURT SYSTEM

First Stop: State Court

Almost all cases (about 95 percent) start in state courts. These courts go by various names, depending on the state in which they operate: circuit, district, municipal, county, or superior courts. The case is tried and decided by a judge, a panel of judges, or a jury.

The side that loses can then appeal to the next level.

First Stop: Federal Court

U.S. DISTRICT COURT—About 5 percent of cases begin their journey in federal court. Most of these cases concern federal laws, the U.S. Constitution, or disputes that involve two or more states. They are heard in one of the ninety-four U.S. District Courts in the nation.

U.S. COURT OF INTERNATIONAL TRADE—Federal court cases involving international trade appear in the U.S. Court of International Trade.

U.S. CLAIMS COURT—The U.S. Claims Court hears federal cases that involve more than $10,000, American Indian claims, and some disputes with government contractors.

The loser in federal court can appeal to the next level.

Appeals: State Cases

Forty states have appeals courts that hear cases that have come from the state courts. In states without an appeals court, the case goes directly to the state supreme court.

Appeals: Federal Cases

U.S. CIRCUIT COURT—Cases appealed from U.S. district courts go to U.S. Circuit Courts of Appeals. There are twelve circuit courts that handle cases from throughout the nation. Each district court and every state and territory are assigned to one of the twelve circuits. Appeals in a few state cases—those that deal with rights guaranteed by the U.S. Constitution—are also heard in this court.

U.S. COURT OF APPEALS—Cases appealed from the U.S. Court of International Trade and the U.S. Claims Court are heard by the U.S. Court of Appeals for the Federal Circuit. Among the cases heard in this court are those involving patents and minor claims against the federal government.

Further Appeals: State Supreme Court

Cases appealed from state appeals courts go to the highest courts in the state—usually called supreme court. In New York, the state's highest court is called the court of appeals. Most state cases do not go beyond this point.

Final Appeals: U.S. Supreme Court

The Supreme Court is the highest court in the country. Its decision on a case is the final word. The Court decides issues that can affect every person in the nation. It has decided cases on slavery, abortion, school segregation, and many other important issues.

The Court selects the cases it will hear—usually around one hundred each year. Four of the nine justices must vote to consider a case in order for it to be heard. Almost all cases have been appealed from the lower courts (either state or federal).

Most people seeking a decision from the Court submit a petition for certiorari. Certiorari means that the case will be moved from a lower court to a higher court for review. The Court receives about seven thousand of these requests annually. The petition outlines the case and gives reasons why the Court should review it.

In rare cases, for example *New York Times* v. *United*

States, an issue must be decided immediately. When such a case is of national importance, the Court allows it to bypass the usual lower court system and hears the case directly.

To win a spot on the Court's docket, a case must fall within one of the following categories:

- Disputes between states and the federal government or between two or more states. It also reviews cases involving ambassadors, consuls, and foreign ministers.
- Appeals from a state court that has ruled on a federal question.
- Appeals from federal appeals courts (about two-thirds of all requests fall into this category).

opinions that must be resolved? If four or more of the nine justices support the request for certiorari, the Court will hear the case.

In the fall of 1973, the Court considered whether to grant certiorari to *DeFunis* v. *Odegaard*. Attorneys for the two sides turned in briefs, written summaries of why the Court should or should not grant certiorari. Marco DeFunis was the petitioner—he had petitioned, or requested, the Court to review the case. His attorney argued that the Court should hear *DeFunis* v. *Odegaard* because the case concerned two important questions. The first dealt with the Constitution: "Is the affirmative action program in violation of the 'Equal Protection' clause [of the Fourteenth Amendment] because preference is given to certain racial minorities?" The second concerned federal law: "Is Title VI of the 1964 Civil Rights Act violated because white applicants must meet different and more stringent standards than persons of other races in obtaining admissions?"

The University of Washington law school was the respondent in the case—its role was to respond to the petitioner's charges. The university did not want the Court to grant certiorari in *DeFunis* v. *Odegaard*. From UWLS's point of view, the decision of the Washington State Supreme Court was correct and should remain in force. Attorney Gorton, representing UWLS, wrote the brief against certiorari. He argued that the key question in the case was: "May UWLS constitutionally take into account, as one element in selecting from among qualified candidates for the study of law, the race of applicants in pursuit of a state policy to mitigate gross under-representation of certain minorities in the law school, and in the membership of the bar?" That question, according to Gorton, had already been sufficiently answered by previous cases and did not need to be brought before the Court.

Once the justices had reviewed the briefs, they had to vote on whether or not to grant certiorari—in other words, whether the Court would hear the case. Four justices voted against it. They felt that the case was moot, or lacking in practical meaning, because DeFunis had already begun his third and final year of law school and would probably graduate from UWLS before the case was decided. One justice, Lewis F. Powell, was undecided. The remaining four voted to grant certiorari, giving *DeFunis* v. *Odegaard* its place on the Supreme Court docket. One of the justices who voted for certiorari was Douglas, who during the previous summer had granted the stay of action against the state supreme court's ruling. Douglas's law clerk—one of the highly regarded and influential lawyers who assist the justices by reviewing cases, summarizing legal points, and writing first drafts of documents—had pointed out to him that the "controversy will continue and is a recurring one." The clerk added that if the justices dismissed the case as moot, "I think it would be fairly obvious that all the court is doing is ducking the issue."

Next, the petitioner and the respondent submitted longer, more detailed briefs to the justices. These set forth each side's views on the points of law at issue. The brief for DeFunis focused on the equal protection clause of the Fourteenth Amendment. It argued that UWLS had violated equal protection in two ways. First, it had given preference to some people "solely on the basis of race" in the competition for "limited spaces available in law school." Second, it had used stricter standards for whites than for persons of color. The brief claimed that the Washington State Supreme Court decision had failed to find a "compelling interest" that would justify the state in overriding Fourteenth Amendment protection. It concluded, "Individual rights cannot be flagrantly sacrificed in the interest of achieving racial balance. Past inequities are not corrected by creating new inequities. . . ."

Slade Gorton's brief for UWLS emphasized the difference between harmful discrimination and helpful, affirmative discrimination, arguing that the Fourteenth Amendment prohibited only the former. UWLS's admissions policy was meant to diversify, enhance, and improve education, the legal profession, and society in general—a goal that gave the state a compelling interest in supporting it.

Although Marco DeFunis and the University of Washington Law School were the primary parties in the case, many others were deeply interested in it. Some were individuals who felt that their experiences and positions gave them something significant to say—on one side of the case or the other—about racial preferences, affirmative action, or minority admissions. Some were groups concerned that the outcome of the case would affect their members. When the Court is preparing to hear a case, an outside party with an interest in the matter may file a brief with the Court as an *amicus curiae*, or friend of the Court. Amicus briefs typically state an individual's or group's arguments for or against a position. They may call the justices' attention to certain facts or emphasize the scope, possible effects, and significance of the case. *DeFunis* v. *Odegaard* generated thirty amicus briefs. This unusually large number indicated that the case was widely viewed as important. It was also controversial—so controversial that it pitted former allies against one another. Groups that had once supported each other now filed amicus briefs on opposite sides of *DeFunis* v. *Odegaard*.

Twenty-two of the amicus briefs filed in the case supported the UWLS position. They represented more than 120 organizations and individuals, many of whom had pooled their voices in combined briefs. Among them were government bodies, including the city of Seattle and the U.S. Equal Employment Opportunity Commission; professional and educational groups, including the American Bar Association, the Council on Legal Education, the American Association of Medical Colleges, and the National Education Association; and civil rights groups, including the NAACP, the SCLC, and the National Organization for Women. The primary argument of most of these briefs was that the end justified the means. American society had a compelling interest in counteracting the national history of racial discrimination, even if doing so meant allowing temporary racial preferences. Wrote Marian Wright Edelman of the Children's Defense Fund, "Color-blindness has come to represent the long-term goal. It is now well understood, however, that our society cannot be completely color-blind in the short term if we are to have a color-blind society in the long term."

The *DeFunis* case split the liberal, progressive wing of American political life. Organizations that had fought together for civil rights during the 1960s—and sometimes marched side by side in the streets of Southern cities to win equality for African Americans—now found themselves in disagreement. In the *DeFunis* case, the National Council of Jewish Women sided with the NAACP and other civil-rights groups to support UWLS's policy of preferential admissions, but other Jewish organizations filed amicus briefs in support of DeFunis. These groups were not against schools using affirmative action to recruit more minority students, as long as those students were qualified and were judged by the same standards as others; however, they opposed policies that used quotas, numerical goals, and set-asides. The brief submitted by the Jewish Rights Council, for example, argued that academic excellence should be the essential factor in school admissions: "The merit system of admissions to institutions of higher learning has been one of the keystones for the success of the Jew and other minorities in America." Among the other groups that filed amicus briefs on the side of DeFunis and against affirmative action were the U.S. Chamber of Commerce, the National Association of Manufacturers, the AFL-CIO (one of the nation's largest labor unions), and the Advocate Society, which included a number of Polish-, Italian-, and Jewish-American groups.

The next step of the Supreme Court process was the oral arguments, which took place February 26, 1974. Oral arguments before the justices follow a highly structured pattern. The lawyers for each side of the case have exactly thirty minutes in which to present their arguments to the panel of justices, who often interrupt with questions or comments. When an attorney has reached the twenty-five-minute mark, a white light comes on to signal that only five minutes remain. At the end of the half hour, a red light comes on to tell the attorney to stop talking and sit down. The process is so different from anything else in the American court system that attorneys who come before the Supreme Court for the first time receive a printed guide to the procedure. The guide also contains tips on etiquette for the occasion, such as "never under any circumstances interrupt a Justice" and "Attempts at humor usually fall flat."

On the day of the *DeFunis* v. *Odegaard* oral arguments, the courtroom was filled with spectators. Diamond, DeFunis's attorney, spoke first. He stated that UWLS's admissions policy created two classes, minority students and nonminority students, and that the two groups received different treatment, which was unconstitutional. Next, Gorton argued on behalf of UWLS. He admitted that the school's admissions policy showed racial preference but claimed that the affirmative action was constitutional because it was not harmful and that it served a greater social good. Each attorney's presentation was interrupted by numerous questions from the justices. That evening and the following morning, news broadcasts and newspapers reported that the oral arguments had taken place. Across the land, from the campus of the University of Washington to the halls of government in Washington, D.C., people who cared about *DeFunis* v. *Odegaard* wondered how long it would take for the Court to reach its decision and what that decision would be.

Four days later, the justices met in a closed conference session to discuss the case. They had two points to discuss—not just whether the admissions policy at UWLS violated the Fourteenth Amendment, but also whether they should consider the question moot, or lacking in significance. Months earlier, when granting certiorari to the case, the justices had narrowly voted that it *wasn't* moot.

Legal Language

The law and the court system often seem to have a language all their own. Although it can appear confusing, legal terminology serves a purpose: It is concise and precise, intended to reduce the possibility of misunderstanding. Much of it, however, is also technical, unfamiliar to the ordinary person, and old-fashioned, carried down from old Roman and English laws and legal practices. Few people without legal training understand the specialized language of the law. This glossary explains some terms connected with lawsuits, court procedures, and affirmative action cases.

Affirmative action: Institutions such as schools and employers taking active steps to counteract the effects of past discrimination against minorities and women.

Amicus curiae: "Friend of the court" (from Latin). A person or organization that is not part of a law case but who has an interest in the outcome and submits a brief to the court in support of one side or the other.

Appeal: To take a case to a higher court to be reheard. The party who loses a lawsuit may appeal the decision to the next level in the court system—for example, from a state court to an appeals or appellate court (if that state has this level), from an appellate court to the state supreme court, and from a state supreme court to the U.S. Supreme Court.

Brief: Document setting forth arguments in a law case.

Certiorari, **writ of:** Order that a higher court grants when it agrees to hear a case appealed from a lower court.

Compelling interest: A reason for the state to do something. A compelling interest should be an important goal that cannot be achieved by any other means. (Here, "state" means a state government, the federal government, or a government-supported institution, such as a state university.)

Complainant: The one who makes a complaint or brings a case to the courts. Also called a **Plaintiff**. See **Petitioner**.

Constitutionality: The question of whether an action is permitted under the U.S. Constitution or is in violation of it. Questions of constitutionality are decided by the U.S. Supreme Court.

Defendant or **defense:** The one against whom a complaint is made; the side that defends against a lawsuit. See **Respondent**.

Discrimination: Act of singling out a group or groups of people for worse treatment than others receive, or judging them by different standards.

Dissent: Disagreement or departure from the majority opinion. Justices who disagree with a majority ruling of the Court may write dissenting opinions that explain their positions.

Due process: A right guaranteed to all citizens under the Fifth and Fourteenth Amendments of the Constitution, which state that the law will be applied to all citizens in the same way, in all circumstances.

Equal protection: A right guaranteed to all citizens under the Fourteenth Amendment of the Constitution, which says that all citizens must receive the same protection of the laws, regardless of race, color, creed, or the fact that they were formerly slaves.

Intermediate scrutiny: Degree of examination that is less demanding than **Strict scrutiny**; often applied to questions of **Constitutionality**.

Majority: In Supreme Court cases, five out of nine justices. See **Swing vote**.

Moot: Without practical significance. A court may decide that a case is moot if a decision will be meaningless or have no effect; in law school, students practice by arguing cases in mock or moot court.

Petitioner: Party who brings a case before the U.S. Supreme Court. See **Complainant**.

Plaintiff: See **Complainant**.

Precedent: Principle established in a previous law case or cases; new cases are often decided on the basis of the precedent set by earlier ones.

Quota: A set, specific percentage or amount.

Respondent: Second party in a Supreme Court case. See **Defendant**.

Reverse discrimination: The idea that affirmative action measures to aid the victims of former discrimination, such as minorities and women, discriminate against whites and men.

Statutory: Having to do with the law.

Strict scrutiny: The strictest or most thorough examination of an action, law, or policy. Justices often apply strict scrutiny to questions about violations of individual rights, or about whether the government has a compelling interest. See **Intermediate scrutiny**.

Swing vote: The tiebreaker, or vote that settles a tie between four Supreme Court justices on one side and four on the other.

Unanimous: Agreed to by all. In Supreme Court cases, a unanimous decision, with all nine justices in agreement, is considered more emphatic than a split decision; a unanimous decision, however, has no more legal force than a simple majority.

The day before the oral arguments, however, they had received word that Marco DeFunis had enrolled in classes for his final quarter of law school at UWLS. It was almost unimaginable that the school would dismiss him now. Did this mean that the Court had no need to hear his case?

At this point, the question of mootness required a majority vote, or five justices. Four of the justices—Potter Stewart, Harry Blackmun, William Rehnquist, and Chief Justice Warren E. Burger—voted to declare the case moot. Four others—Douglas, William J. Brennan Jr., Thurgood Marshall, and Byron White—voted against mootness. They felt that the Court should decide the case, not dismiss it as moot.

THE SUPREME COURT JUSTICES IN A 1972 PORTRAIT: (FRONT, LEFT TO RIGHT) POTTER STEWART, WILLIAM O. DOUGLAS, WARREN E. BURGER, WILLIAM J. BRENNAN JR., BRYON R. WHITE; (REAR, LEFT TO RIGHT) LEWIS F. POWELL, THURGOOD MARSHALL, HARRY A. BLACKMUN, WILLIAM H. REHNQUIST. THIS GROUP OF JUSTICES HEARD BOTH THE *DeFUNIS* AND *BAKKE* CASES, TWO TESTS OF AFFIRMATIVE ACTION IN HIGHER EDUCATION.

Powell, destined to be the tiebreaker, was undecided. The justices agreed to await his decision. Two weeks later, he delivered it. Although it disturbed him to know that many people would accuse the Court of avoiding a difficult issue, Powell cast his vote for mootness. The Supreme Court, in other words, issued the majority opinion that the case of *DeFunis* v. *Odegaard* was without legal significance. Even though the case stemmed from Marco DeFunis's rejection from law school, he would soon graduate from law school with or without a Court ruling on the merits of his case.

The four justices who disagreed with the vote for mootness issued a separate, dissenting opinion. Brennan, who wrote it, criticized the Court for what he called "sidestepping" an important issue. In addition, Douglas issued a dissenting opinion of his own, in which he addressed the question of the constitutionality of UWLS's preferential admissions policy. In Douglas's view, the policy was unconstitutional. He interpreted the Fourteenth Amendment to mean that race should not work against *or* for an individual. However, Douglas's view had no effect on the law or on the case of *DeFunis* v. *Odegaard*.

The *DeFunis* case was over. In the dissenting opinion, though, Justice Brennan had written that the issue of affirmative action and preferential admissions "will not disappear." The question, he predicted, would come before the Supreme Court again. Brennan was right—and it didn't take long. Four years after the justices ruled *DeFunis* v. *Odegaard* moot, they would have to deal with *University of California Regents* v. *Bakke*, and this time they would not be able to duck the issue.

four
ALLAN BAKKE
GOES TO COURT

THE *DeFunis* and *Bakke* cases were a lot alike. Both were complaints by white men who felt that professional schools had turned them down in favor of less-qualified minority candidates. The two cases were linked by more than the similarity of the complaints. Allan Bakke was inspired to press his lawsuit in part by the example of Marco DeFunis's case—and by a meeting with a university official who proved to be an unlikely ally.

After the University of California at Davis medical school had rejected Allan Bakke's application for the 1973–1974 year, Bakke wrote twice to Dr. George Lowrey, dean of admissions for UCDMS.

ALLAN BAKKE'S DETERMINATION TO BECOME A DOCTOR GAVE RISE TO A COURT CASE THAT RAISED THE ISSUE OF "REVERSE DISCRIMINA-TION." BAKKE CLAIMED THAT A POLICY MEANT TO HELP MINORITIES HAD DISCRIMINATED AGAINST HIM.

In his second letter, dated July 1, 1973, Bakke raised the possibility that he might challenge UCDMS's affirmative action admissions policy in court. The letter ended, "I do still hope to be admitted to medical school. I won't quit trying."

Bakke didn't quit trying. The following month, he applied for a second time to UCDMS. Now he was seeking early admission for the 1974–1975 year. Although less than nine months had passed since his first application, things were different this time.

One difference was that UCDMS's procedures for receiving applications and interviewing candidates had changed slightly. UCDMS now belonged to the American Medical College Application System (AMCAS). Students hoping to go to medical school had to complete only one application, and AMCAS would then send it to every school in which they were interested. This made applying to medical schools easier, which in turn meant a big jump in the number of applications that UCDMS received. For the 1974–1975 year, the school received more than 3,737 applications, up almost 1,200, or about 50 percent, from the previous year. The number of available places, however, remained unchanged: 100. Sixteen of those were reserved for minority applications, leaving eighty-four seats to be filled from among more than 3,100 non-minority candidates.

The application form that Bakke had completed in his first attempt to get into UCDMS had given students the opportunity to identify themselves as economically or educationally disadvantaged, but it had not specifically asked about race. The new form, however, specifically asked whether applicants who wished to be considered as "economically and/or educationally disadvantaged" belonged to one of four racial minorities: black, Chicano, Asian, and American Indian. Applications from candidates who placed themselves in the disadvantaged category went to the special admissions subcommittee, or task force. In 1973, 73 white candidates had identified themselves as disadvantaged. In 1974, that number rose to 172. The task force reviewed none of their applications. It had never admitted a white candidate to UCDMS through the special admissions process.

Of course, Allan Bakke did not place himself in the special-admissions category. In fact, by the time his application for 1974–1975 reached UCDMS, members of the admissions committee knew who Bakke was. They were aware that he had recently threatened to sue the school over racial preferences in admissions. By this time, also, Bakke had established a relationship with someone inside the committee.

surprising support

Peter Storandt was an assistant to Lowrey, the head of admissions. The son of an admissions officer at Cornell University in New York State, Storandt was thirty years old in the summer of 1973. He had worked in the admissions offices of Wayne State University's medical school and the Medical College of Pennsylvania before coming to work at UCDMS in 1972. In his short time at UCDMS, Storandt, who had once considered becoming a doctor, had grown concerned about his employer's admissions policy. "We had a program with a supportable aim," he would say later, referring to the aim of counteracting past discrimination through affirmative action, "but . . . it had the effect of bringing hardship on other kinds of candidates. I couldn't be fully comfortable with that kind of arrangement." Storandt described himself as "stubbornly fair-minded." In his view, a policy that favored racial identity over grades, test scores, and other evidence of hard work and determination was simply not fair. He was particularly troubled by the fact that the task force had never admitted a white disadvantaged candidate. The admissions policy, as he saw it, had flaws.

To make matters worse, Storandt's job required him to field questions from candidates who were disappointed at being rejected. He felt that, on the question of admissions and rejections, the school wasn't completely straightforward with applicants, whether black or white, special or regular admission. He had already raised this point more than once with the UCDMS administrators.

When Lowrey received Allan Bakke's second letter of complaint about his rejection, he gave Storandt the job of answering the letter. Storandt reviewed the file on Bakke before he wrote back to the disappointed candidate. What he saw in the file tied in with the misgivings he'd been feeling for some time. Bakke appeared to Storandt to have "a sterling record and top scores." Storandt was deeply disturbed at having to tell such a candidate that he couldn't get into medical school when, Storandt knew, some candidates had been admitted by the task force in spite of school records that revealed what he called "academic difficulty." Storandt then communicated with Bakke, as Lowrey had asked him to do. The content and the results of his communication, however, were certainly not what Lowrey or UCDMS had in mind.

"Dear Allan," Storandt began, and went on to write a
long letter giving considerably more information than was
strictly necessary. Storandt told Bakke that he had placed
high in the overall ranking of applicants for 1973–1974.
He'd had to be turned down, however, because there simply wasn't room for all the "remarkably able and well-
qualified individuals" who had applied. Storandt also said
that Bakke's age was not a barrier to attending UCDMS,
pointing out that "older applicants have successfully
entered and worked in our curriculum." He also encour-
aged Bakke to apply to UCDMS for the 1974–1975 year,
under the early admissions plan and using the newly
adopted AMCAS form. If Bakke applied soon, UCDMS
would be able to let him know no later than October 1, 1973,
whether he had been admitted for the following year.

So far, Storandt's letter was probably about what
Lowrey had expected his assistant to produce: something
to soothe and reassure an angry, impatient candidate.
But in the second half of his letter, Storandt went beyond
the scope of his duties. If UCDMS turned Bakke down a
second time, Storandt suggested, Bakke could then
"pursue your research on quota-oriented minority
recruiting." Storandt enclosed a page that contained the
official description of the special admissions policy at
UCDMS, saying, "I don't know whether you would consider our program to have the overtones of a quota or not
. . . but the fact remains that most applicants to such a
program are members of ethnic minority groups."
Storandt also suggested that Bakke research the *DeFunis*
case, which had been presented to the U.S. Supreme
Court. Finally, Storandt suggested that Bakke contact

two medical school officials, one in Arizona and one in New York, who might be able to tell him more about the legal aspects of minority admissions.

Several weeks later, Bakke met with Storandt on the UCDMS campus. Over coffee, Storandt answered a flurry of questions about the special admissions policy. He gave Bakke information that was not contained in the official description. Bakke learned that although white candidates had applied to UCDMS under special admissions, none had ever been admitted through the task force. He also learned that some minority candidates had been accepted with scores lower than his own, and that the number of places reserved for special admissions candidates each year was set at sixteen.

Bakke wrote to Storandt the following week, thanking the official for meeting with him. "I appreciate your interest," Bakke told Storandt, "in the moral and legal propriety of quotas and preferential admissions policies; even more impressive to me was your real concern about the effect of admissions policies on each individual applicant." In the letter, Bakke said he intended to apply to several medical schools, including UCDMS, for the following year. He also wrote of his willingness to try "a legal challenge" to racial admissions quotas. Storandt wrote back to Bakke on August 15, 1973, saying, "It seems to me that you have carefully arranged your thinking about this matter and that the eventual result of your next actions will be of significance to many present and future medical students." Clearly, Storandt recognized the likelihood of a lawsuit from Bakke.

But what role, if any, did Storandt play in Bakke's decision to sue Storandt's employer for reverse discrimination? Four years later, as the U.S. Supreme Court wrestled with *University of California Regents* v. *Bakke* and the case was big news in California and across the country, a San Francisco newspaper printed the headline "UC Official Suggested *Bakke* Suit." Storandt gave his own version, with a careful but subtle distinction: "My main view is that I didn't actually encourage the suit—I suggested that it could be pursued." But Storandt also admitted, "I overstepped my bound of propriety and authority" in his dealings with Bakke. Storandt's communications with Bakke may well have turned Bakke's thoughts about possible legal action into a firm plan to sue.

Rejection and Resistance

Following Storandt's advice, Bakke looked up information about Marco DeFunis's reverse discrimination lawsuit against the University of Washington law school. Bakke then wrote to DeFunis, who sent him copies of the briefs and documents that had been filed with the courts in the *DeFunis* case. Bakke followed Storandt's other advice, too, and applied for early admission to UCDMS for the 1974–1975 year. He acted so promptly that his application was already under review when Storandt wrote his letter of August 15.

The AMCAS form was not the only new feature of UDCMS's admissions policy in the fall of 1973. The interviewing and scoring methods had also changed. Likely candidates now had two interviews, one with a faculty member or administrator and the other with a student on the admissions committee. Each candidate's application was reviewed by six members of the committee, and each reviewer gave the candidate a numerical score based on the application and summaries of the interviews. The maximum score from each reviewer was one hundred, for a total benchmark score of six hundred.

Later, a series of courts would examine the scores given to Bakke by the six committee members who reviewed his file. They would also look at the notes taken by his interviewers. Bakke's two interviews took place at the UCDMS campus on August 30. Frank Goia, the student who interviewed Bakke, found the candidate "friendly, well-tempered, conscientious and delightful to speak with." Bakke had explained "that he was not out to sue anybody but that he simply wished to question the logic behind [preferential admissions] policies." Goia gave Bakke "a sound recommendation" for admission to the medical school. Bakke's second interview was with Lowrey, who claimed that it was simply coincidence that he, the dean of admissions, wound up interviewing this potentially troublesome candidate. Lowrey's view of Bakke was less favorable than Goia's. Lowrey described Bakke as "a rather rigidly oriented young man who has the tendency to arrive at conclusions based more upon his personal impressions than upon thoughtful processes using available sources of information." Lowrey's report on the interview also emphasized Bakke's criticisms of the school's special admissions program. Bakke was, Lowrey concluded, "acceptable but certainly not an outstanding candidate for our medical school."

The six scores given to Bakke's application varied considerably. Storandt was one of the scorers; he gave Bakke 92 out of a possible 100 points. Three other committee members rated Bakke at 96, 94, and 87. Of the two committee members who had interviewed Bakke, Goia gave the candidate 94 points, while Lowrey gave him his lowest score, 86. Together, Bakke's scores totaled 549 out of a possible 600.

By the end of September 1973, Bakke knew that he had been rejected under the early admissions program. His application went into the general pool to be reconsidered the following spring. It must have been an anxious, suspenseful winter for Bakke, but on April 1, 1974, he received a form letter from UCDMS that ended the suspense. He had been turned down again.

Determination comes across strongly in Bakke's letters and applications. Faced with his second rejection from UCDMS, he didn't lose that determination. As set on attending medical school as ever, Bakke had already begun planning for his next step. Four months earlier, he had met with San Francisco attorney Reynold Colvin to talk about the possibility of suing the medical school.

A few years earlier, Colvin had been part of an affirmative action case in federal district court. Colvin had represented school administrators who protested against a policy that, in a time of severe budget cuts, protected the job status and promotion prospects of minority employees over whites. The decision in *Anderson* v. *S. F. Unified School District* was a victory for Colvin. The judge ruled the policy illegal, saying, "Preferential treatment under the guise of 'affirmative action' is the imposition of one form of racial discrimnation in place of another. . . . No one race or ethnic group should ever be accorded preferential treatment over another. . . . There is no place for racial groupings in America. Only in individual accomplishment can equality be achieved." Both

DeFunis and Bakke would have agreed heartily with this judge's decision. It was through DeFunis, in fact, that Bakke found Colvin. The material that DeFunis had sent to Bakke contained a reference to Colvin's victory against the San Francisco school board.

FIRST STEP, MIXED RESULTS

At their first meeting, in January 1974, Colvin warned Bakke that seeing a lawsuit through the court system is a long, difficult process. He advised Bakke to wait until the U.S. Supreme Court had delivered its decision on *DeFunis* v. *Odegaard.* That decision should answer the question of whether preferential admissions were allowable in higher education. A few months later, however, the Supreme Court dismissed *DeFunis* as moot without delivering a decision. The question was still up in the air, and so was Allan Bakke's future. Bakke, who had just received his second rejection from UCDMS, contacted Colvin again. The lawsuit was on.

Because Bakke cared much more about attending medical school than about creating a case to settle an issue, Colvin's first step was to see whether he could convince UCDMS to reconsider its rejection—in other words, to make an exception for Bakke and somehow squeeze him into the class of 1974–1975. University officials thought about doing this, but they decided that it might open the door to too much pressure from other rejected candidates, so they said no.

On June 20, 1974, Colvin filed Bakke's lawsuit against the University of California in Superior Court of Yolo County, home of UCDMS. Colvin chose this state court instead of the federal district court in San Francisco because he believed the state court would be more likely to respond to his mission of getting Allan Bakke into medical school, while a federal court might see the case as an impersonal question of legal points. The Yolo County suit wasn't a passionate courtroom drama. It unfolded as a series of papers filed by each side and reviewed by a judge.

Colvin's complaint charged that his client was qualified for medical school but had been prevented from attending because UCDMS had set a quota of 16 percent for minority students. Under that quota, minority applicants were judged by special standards, and some had been admitted who had lower test scores and grades than Bakke. Colvin argued that Bakke's rights had been violated under the California state constitution, the Fourteenth Amendment of the U.S. Constitution, and Title VI of the Civil Rights Act of 1964, which says that no program that receives federal funds can exclude anyone because of race. Colvin asked the judge to order UCDMS to admit Bakke.

Attorney Donald Reidhaar represented the University of California. He responded to Colvin's complaint by arguing that even without the special admissions program, Bakke would not have won admission to UCDMS. (Thirty-two candidates with higher scores than Bakke's, all of them white, had also failed to get in for the 1974–1975 year.) Reidhaar then broadened the scope of the case beyond the question of whether or not UCDMS should admit Allan Bakke. He asked the court to declare that UCDMS's special admissions program was constitutional. The university and its lawyers were seeking clear guidelines. They wanted the court to resolve the questions that had been raised about preferential admissions for minorities. Of course, they thought the judge's decision would support their program.

More months of waiting passed. In November of 1974, Judge F. Leslie Manker issued his ruling. The judge found that UCDMS's special admissions program was illegal. It was a quota system, with 16 percent of places reserved for candidates who were chosen by race and who competed with each other, not with all other candidates. "No race or ethnic group," wrote Manker, "should ever be granted privileges or immunities not given to every other race." To Bakke's disappointment, however, Manker did not order UCDMS to admit him, as the Washington court had ordered UWLS to admit Marco DeFunis to law school. Bakke, ruled Manker, had not proved that he would have gotten in if sixteen places hadn't been set aside for special admissions. The judge merely ordered UCDMS to review Bakke's application again, this time with no consideration of race.

No one was happy with this outcome. As Colvin put it, "both sides lost." Bakke was unhappy that he couldn't start medical school. The university was dismayed that its affirmative action program had been declared illegal. It was even more dismayed a few months later when, after Colvin presented additional arguments, Judge Manker changed his initial ruling. He issued an order that prohibited UCDMS from using race as any kind of factor in admissions, and he also shifted the burden of proof to UCDMS. Instead of Bakke having to prove that he *would* have gotten in if there were no task force, the school now had to prove that he would *not* have been admitted. This was difficult to do. Numbers and statistics were available for comparing the scores of special admissions, regular admissions, and rejected candidates. One feature of the admissions process, though, was never openly discussed during the case, although Peter Storandt and others had previously questioned it. That was the practice of allowing the dean of the medical school, Dr. C. John Tupper, to "recommend" candidates for admission based on factors other than merit. Many of these handpicked candidates had socially prominent parents, such as politicians or people who gave large sums of money to the school. In some years, as many as five seats in the entering class at UCDMS went to Tupper's "recommendations." Because of such exceptions, and because the admissions guidelines were somewhat open to personal interpretation, neither side could say with certainty that Bakke would or would not have gotten into UCDMS if there had been no special admissions program.

surprise in state supreme court

With neither side satisfied, the next step for *University of California Regents* v. *Bakke* was an appeal to a higher court. In May 1975, both Reidhaar and Colvin asked the California Supreme Court to hear the case. The court said that it would do so, recognizing that this was a case of broad importance. One staff member of the court later recalled, "All of the justices . . . agreed that it was an issue which needed to be faced head-on."

The California Supreme Court was no stranger to controversy. Widely regarded as liberal and progressive, it had gone further than the U.S. Supreme Court in such measures as banning the death penalty and extending rights to the poor, to criminal suspects, and to minorities.

According to reporter Joel Dreyfuss and legal scholar Charles Lawrence III, "This was a court that was viewed as a champion of the underdog and that gloried in its activist reputation." Supporters of affirmative action in education no doubt expected the court to overturn, or reverse, the Yolo County court's ruling.

By now, the case was drawing some media attention in the press, at least in California. Nine organizations filed amicus briefs with the state supreme court, representing the views and interests of their members. Three of them supported Bakke and opposed quotas. They were the American Federation of Teachers, the American Jewish Congress, and the Anti-Defamation League of B'nai B'rith. Six groups—medical and law school associations, along with the NAACP and other civil rights organizations—supported the University of California and its special admissions program.

Oral arguments took place before the seven justices of the court in March 1976. Each side presented basically the same arguments it had used in superior court. Colvin made the point that racial discrimination was acceptable only as a *direct* remedy, or correction, for past wrongs. UCDMS could not use racial discrimination to help minorities because there was no record that UCDMS had ever used it to harm them. Reidhaar emphasized the difference between harmful and benign discrimination, claiming that benign discrimination was allowable. The question of whether Bakke would or would not have been admitted to UCDMS in the absence of special minority admissions remained unanswered.

Six months later, the court delivered its ruling. By a six to one majority, it agreed with Judge Manker's earlier ruling that UCDMS's policy created an illegal system of racial quotas. The goal of increasing the number of minority medical students and doctors was admirable and served the interests of the state, but the UCDMS policy was an unsuitable way to achieve that goal. Having examined the policy under the strict scrutiny standard—the most demanding level of scrutiny, often used in questions of civil rights and compelling state interest—the court found that the policy was not "narrowly tailored" enough. The school, in other words, could have used other methods to increase diversity, methods that would not have violated anyone's civil rights. The verdict was that UCDMS had violated Bakke's rights under the Fourteenth Amendment (the court did not address the California State Constitution or the Civil Rights Act of 1964). In addition, the supreme court remanded, or sent back, *University of California Regents* v. *Bakke* to

Yolo County Superior Court for a determination on the question of whether UCDMS had to admit Allan Bakke. This meant that UCDMS had to do one of two things: produce proof that Bakke wouldn't have been admitted in any case, or admit him.

The court's decision shocked and deeply disappointed supporters of affirmative action. One state supreme court justice, Mathew O. Tobriner, shared their feelings. Tobriner pointed out that all of the minority candidates who had graduated from UCDMS were fully qualified to practice medicine. There was no evidence that Allan Bakke would

CALIFORNIA STATE SUPREME COURT JUSTICE MATTHEW O. TOBRINER WROTE THE DISSENTING OPINION IN THE CALIFORNIA SUPREME COURT HEARING OF THE *BAKKE* CASE, ARGUING IN FAVOR OF AFFIRMATIVE ACTION.

have made a better doctor than any one of them. Society had a duty to counteract its all-too-real racial inequalities, and programs that offset the imbalances of the past were one way of doing so.

Tobriner had argued "very loudly and long and strenuously" with his fellow justices, as he later said, but he was unable to win any of them over to his position. In the end, he wrote a fifty-seven-page dissenting opinion in which he declared, "Two centuries of slavery and racial discrimination have left our nation an awful legacy, a largely separated society in which wealth, educational resources, employment opportunities—indeed all of society's benefits—remain largely the preserve of the white-Anglo majority." Tobriner added that it was sad and ironic that the Fourteenth Amendment, which two decades earlier the courts had used to force the nation's elementary and secondary schools to integrate, was now a tool for preventing graduate schools from voluntarily integrating.

TO THE HIGHEST COURT

Once again, no one was happy with the court's decision. Bakke should have been happy: After UCDMS admitted that it couldn't prove that Bakke's rejection had nothing to do with the special admissions program, the state supreme court changed its earlier ruling and ordered the school to admit him at once. This victory for Bakke was short-lived, however. Almost immediately, the university appealed the case to the U.S. Supreme Court, requesting a grant of certiorari. While the Court considered whether or not to grant the request, Assistant Justice William Rehnquist issued a stay, an order that

CALIFORNIA STATE SUPREME COURT JUSTICE STANLEY MOSK WROTE THE MAJORITY OPINION.

put the state supreme court's orders on hold. In similar circumstances, Marco DeFunis had been allowed to attend law school while awaiting the outcome of his case in the highest court. This time, however, circumstances worked against the would-be student. Allan Bakke would have to keep waiting.

Not everyone was pleased to see *University of California Regents* v. *Bakke* headed toward the U.S. Supreme Court. Even before attorney Reidhaar filed the petition for certiorari, a number of groups tried to persuade the university to drop the case and simply live with the California Supreme Court's ruling against the task force program. Surprisingly, these organizations represented minorities. Among them were the National

Organization for Women (NOW), the National Conference of Black Lawyers, and the National Urban League. Why would groups known for their support of minority and civil rights try to keep the University of California from taking its case to the Supreme Court?

Many feared that the university had a weak case. Twice already, the lower courts had ruled that UCDMS's special admissions program was quota-driven and unconstitutional. Was it likely that the Supreme Court, which had become less liberal and stricter about constitutional interpretation in recent years, would disagree? Questions about affirmative action's legality and constitutionality were tremendously important—they could affect the futures of millions of people. Better, some felt, to bring them to the highest court in a stronger case, one that the affirmative action side would have a better chance of winning.

Another factor was that many minority and civil rights groups, as well as people of color, felt isolated from the *Bakke* case, even resentful about it. For years these individuals and groups had planned and led the fight against discrimination. In matters such as school desegregation and equal access to housing, they had fought for civil rights and an end to racism. Now, however, they were on the outside, while a white man and a largely white university went to battle over a key civil-rights issue. Minorities felt that they lacked representation, although the case's outcome deeply concerned them.

Once Reidhaar had petitioned for certiorari on behalf of the university, the U.S. Supreme Court

received amicus briefs on the question of certiorari—
that is, on the question of whether the court should hear
the case. One brief came from a coalition of fifteen civil
rights groups. It argued that the Court should not grant
certiorari because the *Bakke* case "was not a good vehi-
cle for deciding such an important issue." During the
case's journey through the lower courts, the university
had failed to offer key arguments, such as the claim that
doctor-patient relationships would improve if medical
schools produced more black doctors, or that the MCAT
test required of all candidates was racially biased and
therefore should be offset by aggressive affirmative
action. But subjects that had not been introduced earlier could not be considered if the case came to the
Supreme Court. For this reason, groups that wanted to
keep the case out of the Supreme Court argued that it
lacked "a fully developed record."

Colvin, Bakke's attorney, also filed a brief with the
Court. Colvin argued that the Court should refuse certiorari because the California Supreme Court's decision had
been the correct one, based on thoughtful application of
previous constitutional decisions by the U.S. Supreme
Court. There was no need to reopen the matter.

But what did the justices think? They discussed
whether or not to grant certiorari to *Bakke* in December
1976 and again in January 1977. The following month
they voted on the question. Four of them were against
certiorari, but the other five formed a majority. On
February 22, 1977, the U.S. Supreme Court announced
that it would hear the case of *University of California
Regents* v. *Bakke*. Four years after his first application

to the university's medical school at Davis, Bakke was bound for the Supreme Court. By now, however, the case was a subject of national attention, and everyone knew that it was about more than one man. As Justice Lewis F. Powell had predicted a few years earlier in *DeFunis*, affirmative action in education was an issue that wouldn't go away.

Five
THE SUPREME COURT SPEAKS

ON THE NIGHT OF OCTOBER 12, 1977, every major
newscast in the nation mentioned the *Bakke* case. ABC
news anchor Harry Reasoner declared, "One of the most
important civil rights cases in two decades, the Allan
Bakke reverse discrimination suit, was argued before the
Supreme Court today." NBC's John Chancellor predicted
that *Bakke* would enter "the Hall of Fame of great cases
which changed the interpretation of the Constitution."
His colleague David Brinkley said that the *Bakke* case was
"one of the most difficult the Court has had in years."
Some newscasters placed the *Bakke* case in the context of
racial history and civil rights law. Carl Stern of NBC, for
example, called *Bakke* perhaps "the most important civil
rights case since segregation was outlawed in the 1950s."

The *Bakke* case was big news that day because the nine
Supreme Court justices had just heard the oral arguments
from both sides. But interest in the case had been building
for some time. So many parties on both sides of the issue
felt concern about *Bakke* that the Supreme Court received
a record number of amicus curiae briefs: 58 in all, representing a total of more than 160 organizations and individuals. The *Los Angeles Times* reported that "never
before in its 189-year history had the nation's highest

court attracted so much unsolicited advice as it received in the Allan Bakke case." Not even *Brown* v. *Board of Education*, the landmark 1954 case that had ended racial segregation in public schools, had drawn so many briefs.

FRIENDS AND FOES

Amicus curiae briefs get their name from the phrase "friends of the court." The strong feelings unleashed by the *Bakke* case, however, meant that the briefs for each side were less than friendly to the opposite side.

Four of the briefs had been filed before certiorari. They concerned the question of whether the Court should hear the case. Of the fifty-four briefs filed after certiorari, thirty-eight sided with the petitioner, the University of California. Repeating many of the arguments raised in the university's own brief, they claimed that UCDMS's affirmative action policy and its special admissions program were legal. They also urged the Supreme Court to reverse the decision of the California Supreme Court.

Among the universities that filed in support of UCDMS were Harvard, long seen as one of the country's most prestigious schools, and Howard, a respected black university. The university briefs raised an issue that had not been addressed in the lower courts—the importance of preserving schools' independence in the matter of admissions. To function properly, these briefs claimed, schools must continue to regulate themselves; they cannot become tools of the state.

Student groups also filed their support for UCDMS's affirmative action policy. Among these were several organizations for African-American and Native American law students. The American Medical Student Association's brief argued that numerical scores such as MCAT results and grade averages "do not predict either success in medical school, or as a physician," and that such scores were "inappropriate instruments for admission to medical school."

The list of professional and educational associations that sided with the university was long. It included the American Bar Association, the National Council of Churches, the Association of American Medical Colleges, the National Education Association, the American Public Health League, the American Association of University Professors, and many more. Some doctors also filed individual briefs in support of the university.

Civil rights groups that filed briefs for the university included the NAACP, the Equal Employment Advisory Council, and the Lawyers Committee for Civil Rights under Law. The American Civil Liberties Union (ACLU) filed a brief that had been written by three attorneys; one of them was Ruth Bader Ginsburg, who later became a Supreme Court justice. Drawing on a concept that had been used in *Brown* v. *Board of Education*, the ACLU brief argued that UCDMS had not violated the Constitution because Allan Bakke's rejection by the school was not a "stigmatic injury" like the psychological damage that had been suffered by minority children in segregated schools.

Fifteen briefs took the other side of the case, supporting Bakke. They asked the Supreme Court to uphold the California Supreme Court's decision against UCDMS. Among those who took this position were a number of ethnic organizations: Polish American, Italian American, and Jewish. The American Federation of Teachers sided with Bakke, as did the Fraternal Order of Police and the Chamber of Commerce of the United States. Several conservative political groups also filed. Marco DeFunis, who had begun practicing law in Seattle, wrote the brief for one of them, the Young Americans for Freedom.

Some of the pro-Bakke briefs came from individuals. One was written by Timothy Hoy, a junior at Oberlin College who planned to apply to law school. Hoy argued that it was wrong "that I should suffer a burden as great as possible denial of admission to law school for past discrimination I did not commit." Many students, however, disagreed with Hoy's position. They would soon hold "anti-Bakke" demonstrations on campuses across the country and organize a protest march outside the Supreme Court building.

THE FEDERAL GOVERNMENT'S BRIEF

Supreme Court justices have had varied views on the usefulness of amicus curiae briefs. For example, Justice Hugo Black, who served from 1937 to 1971, considered them a good way for the Court to keep in touch with the public interest. He thought that the procedures for submitting briefs should be simplified so that more people and groups would do it. At the other extreme, Justice Felix Frankfurter, a member of the Court from 1939 to 1962, thought it should be harder to submit an amicus brief. In his view, briefs let people use the Court "as a soap-box, or an advertising medium." All justices, however, pay especially close attention to briefs that come from the U.S. Department of Justice. Such a brief represents the federal government's official position on an issue.

Suspense and drama swirled around the writing of the government's *Bakke* brief. President Jimmy Carter had taken office just a month before the Supreme Court agreed to hear *Bakke*. Carter, a Democrat, had pledged to support

affirmative action, and he counted on the continued support of minorities and civil rights groups. Now many of
them looked to him to take a stand in the *Bakke* case.

The federal government can file an amicus brief in any
Supreme Court case it chooses. (The Court can also ask the
government to submit a brief, although it did not do so in
Bakke.) Carter turned the task of preparing the government's brief over to two African-American attorneys who
had been newly appointed to positions in the Department of
Justice. Wade McCree Jr. was the U.S. solicitor general, who
represents the federal government in the Supreme Court.
Drew Days III, who had formerly worked for the Legal Fund
of the NAACP, was the assistant attorney general in charge of
civil rights—in other words, he was a presidential legal advi-
sor and lawyer. These two discovered to their dismay that the
path to an acceptable brief ran through a political minefield.

McCree and Days took a scholarly, careful approach to
the *Bakke* case, treating it not as a political issue but as a
question of law. Their first draft of the brief supported
affirmative action in general but opposed fixed quotas.
This would mean that although the government came out
in favor of affirmative action as a goal, it rejected the
UCDMS preferential admissions program and supported
Allan Bakke's demand to enter medical school. President
Carter's advisors were horrified. Such a position would
outrage many of Carter's supporters, who expected a more
whole-hearted endorsement of preferential admissions.
The Black Congressional Caucus, consisting of African-
American senators and representatives, urged Carter to
support UCDMS all the way. It called the brief "a death
sentence for programs which use race or ethnicity to
achieve integration or equality." Days felt the sting of
being regarded as a traitor by former colleagues at the

PRESIDENT JIMMY CARTER AND FIRST LADY ROSALYNN CARTER AFTER
CARTER'S INAUGURATION ON JANUARY 20, 1977. CARTER, A DEMOCRAT,
HAD PLEDGED TO SUPPORT AFFIRMATIVE ACTION. THE *BAKKE* CASE PUT HIS
ADMINISTRATION TO THE TEST.

NAACP, who asked him, "How's your friend Allan doing?"

To make matters worse, the draft of the brief and the uproar it had caused were leaked to the press, which jumped on the story because *Bakke* was now seen as the biggest case of the coming Court term. Chief Justice Warren Burger complained to McCree about the storm of publicity, saying that the justices felt "improper public pressure when they were about to hear oral arguments." The word came down from the White House to McCree and Days: Rewrite the brief in a way that did not break the president's campaign promises. They did so, and the brief was submitted to the Court just nine days before the date set for oral arguments. The final version of the brief strongly supported affirmative action, opposed "rigid" quotas though it did not give any details on that subject, and argued that there was insufficient evidence in the *Bakke* case to determine whether UCDMS's program was legal or whether Allan Bakke should be admitted to the school. This time, it was the federal government that had ducked the issue.

THe oraL ArGumenTs

By the time *Bakke* was argued in the presence of the Supreme Court justices, the University of California had significantly expanded its legal team. Donald Reidhaar was now assisted by several experts in constitutional law, one of whom had recently served as a law clerk in the Supreme Court. The university had also hired Archibald Cox, a former solicitor general who taught law at Harvard and had considerable experience in the Supreme Court, to present its argument. Allan Bakke's legal team, though, still consisted of Reynold Colvin. Bakke could no longer afford to pay for Colvin's services, but the attorney represented him for free, saying,

"I couldn't leave a case of this type, and Allan wouldn't drop it."

On the morning of October 12, the Court's session began like every other. The clack of the gavel signalled the spectators to stand. The nine justices filed into the courtroom and took their seats at the long mahogany bench. For oral arguments in *Bakke*, each side would get an hour, double the usual length. The extra time was because of the case's importance; Wade McCree would have part of the university's hour in which to state the government's position.

As petitioner, the university went first. Cox, who was clearly at ease before the justices, made three main points. UCDMS had not admitted any unqualified candidates. The school had the right to consider race and ethnicity to remedy past discrimination in society. Finally, schools should not lose the right to select their own students. He also argued that UCDMS's program did not violate the Fourteenth Amendment because it did not discriminate negatively, to keep people out or label them inferior, but rather to advance and include them. Cox closed by reminding the justices that UCDMS's program was "aimed at offsetting the consequences of our long tragic history of discrimination, and achieving greater racial integrity."

McCree spoke next. He emphasized two key points. First, he attacked the argument that only institutions proven to have discriminated in the past should be allowed to correct that discrimination with racial preferences. Such a view made no sense in an era "without barriers to travel." Students from all over the country applied to UCDMS. Who could say that some of them had not been discriminated against in other places? Second, McCree argued in favor of a historical, rather than a strictly literal, interpretation of the Fourteenth Amendment, which says that no one can be denied equal protection of the law. That amendment had become law soon after the Civil War. In McCree's view, the lawmakers had clearly intended to protect the rights of newly freed African Americans. He urged the Court to keep that purpose in mind when determining whether UCDMS's program was in keeping with the Fourteenth Amendment.

Colvin spoke last. His strategy was to focus the Court's attention on the specific case of Allan Bakke, not on the broad constitutional issue. "I am Allan Bakke's attorney, and Allan Bakke is my client," he began, and then he recounted in detail Bakke's quest to get into medical school. Finally Justice Lewis F. Powell interrupted him to say, "We are here . . . primarily to hear a constititional argument. You have devoted 20 minutes to belaboring the facts, if I may say so. I would like help . . . on the constitutional issues."

The next half hour held a few sticky minutes for Colvin, as the justices peppered him with questions. One of the most difficult moments for him came during a spirited exchange with Justice Thurgood Marshall. The only African-American justice, Marshall had formerly served as the chief lawyer for the NAACP. In that position he had planned and carried out a long, complex, and successful legal battle against racial segregation. Marshall remained a fervent supporter of affirmative action and took a critical view of Colvin's arguments. At one point he asked Colvin whether he would take the same position if UCDMS had reserved just one seat, instead of sixteen, for special admissions. Colvin replied that he would and that the number didn't matter. "It is the principle of keeping someone out because of his race that is important," Colvin stated. A few moments later Marshall said, "You are talking about your client's right. Don't these underprivileged people [minorities] have some rights?" Colvin began to answer, saying, "They certainly have the right—" Marshall interrupted him testily: "To eat cake." After that, in exchanges with other justices, Colvin restated his basic position: that "any use of race" is unconstitutional and violates Title VI of the Civil Rights Act of 1964.

The presentations ended at noon, after what reporter Anthony Lewis described in *The New York Times* as "an extraordinarily exciting two hours." Chief Justice Burger declared, "Thank you, gentlemen, the case is submitted"—the traditional formula for closing the oral arguments. Now it was up to the justices, who would make their decision behind closed doors.

AGREEING TO DISAGREE

The first time they met in conference after the *Bakke* arguments, the justices gave their initial reactions and held an informal, preliminary vote on the case. Three of them wanted to reverse the entire California Supreme Court decision, which would make the university the clear winner. Four wanted to uphold the entire California Supreme Court decision, which would ban UCDMS's program and require the school to admit Bakke. One justice, Harry Blackmun, was ill in his home state of Minnesota and couldn't yet give his position. The ninth, Powell, had a mixed reaction: He supported the use of race in university admissions but opposed the UCDMS program, so he wanted to uphold part of the state supreme court decision and overturn another part of it. Furthermore, some

Justice Harry Blackmun wrote a separate opinion on *Bakke*, arguing that though he hoped for a time when the nation would be color-blind, that time hadn't yet arrived, and inequalities must still be taken into consideration.

justices wanted to avoid the issue of constitutionality completely and decide the case on statutory grounds only, interpreting the Civil Rights Act but leaving the Fourteenth Amendment issue alone. Others felt that the Court had to confront the constitutional question. Even those who wanted to address the constitutional question disagreed on whether the Court should use the standard of strict scrutiny or a more relaxed standard in interpreting the Constitution.

The court was clearly split on every aspect of the *Bakke* case. No five-justice majority had emerged, although Blackmun's position was not yet known. In November of 1977, Chief Justice Burger directed the justices to review the case, to discuss it among themselves (usually done through written memos rather than meetings), and to await Blackmun's contribution.

A dozen long memos on the *Bakke* case circulated among the justices that winter. In January 1978, in fact, Powell wrote that his "first impulse was to cringe" when he saw another memo. Some of these documents were witty and passionate, particularly Justice Marshall's memo of April 13, in which he wrote, "I repeat, for next to the last time: the decision in this case depends on whether you view the action of [UCDMS] as admitting certain students or as excluding certain other students. . . . As to this country being a melting pot—either the Negro did not get into the pot, or he did not get melted down. . . . If only the principle of color-blindness had been accepted by the majority in *Plessy* in 1896, we would not be faced with this problem in 1978. . . . We are stuck with this case. We must decide it."

But the spate of memos failed to persuade any of the eight to change his initial position. And Justice Blackmun's delay in making up his mind, even after he returned from Minnesota, postponed the final decision for months. Finally, in May, Blackmun wrote a memo that revealed his position. To the surprise of his more conservative colleagues on the Court, and to the delight of Justice Marshall, Blackmun did not join the four justices who wanted to uphold the California Supreme Court's decision in favor of Bakke. Instead, he sided with the three who wanted to overturn that decision. The result was a three-way split: four justices for Bakke, four for the university, and one (Powell) who agreed with part of each position. Because no position was held by five or more justices, there was no majority opinion in the case. Instead, the opinion of the Court was a plurality, which means that the position that has received the greatest number of votes has received fewer than half of the total possible votes.

Burger gave Powell the challenging task of writing the plurality opinion that would be delivered to the public. Getting the wording right took weeks and led to still more heated exchanges among the justices. Finally, on June 28, 1978, Powell was ready to declare the results in the *Bakke* case. He would read them aloud in the Supreme Court's courtroom. Although the Court does say in advance when its decisions will be read, reporters and newscasters had been waiting for weeks for the conclusion of *Bakke*. Now the Court's term was drawing near an end. Suspecting that the wait was over, observers and media people packed the courtroom.

THE NINE *Bakke* JUSTICES AND THEIR OPINIONS

One of the most significant things about being a justice of the U.S. Supreme Court is that the job can last a long time. Justices are chosen by presidents. Once Congress has confirmed, or accepted, the choice, the justice is appointed to the Court. He or she can stay on the Court until retirement or death. To be considered for the Supreme Court, an attorney must have achieved considerable standing in the field of law. This means that when justices arrive at the Court, they are neither young nor at the start of their careers. Some justices, though, have served on the Court for thirty years or longer. The selection of a new justice to fill an empty seat on the Court is a serious matter because a justice may help shape the composition of the Court—and through it, the law of the land—for decades.

The leanings of the Court shift over time as justices come and go. When a president has the chance to appoint a new justice, the chosen justice typically belongs to the president's own political party. And although there have been exceptions, presidents most often pick justices whose ideas and views are

Here are the nine *Bakke* justices and their final positions in the case:

	Served on Court	Appointed by	UCDMS Program Unlawful
Chief Justice Warren E. Burger	1969–1986	Nixon (Rep)	*
Associate Justice William J. Brennan	1956–1990	Eisenhower (Rep)	
Associate Justice Potter Stewart	1958–1981	Eisenhower (Rep)	*
Associate Justice Byron White	1962–1993	Kennedy (Dem)	
Associate Justice Thurgood Marshall	1967–1991	Johnson (Dem)	
Associate Justice Harry Blackmun	1970–1994	Nixon (Rep)	
Associate Justice Lewis J. Powell	1972–1987	Nixon (Rep)	
Associate Justice John Paul Stevens	1975–	Ford (Rep)	*
Associate Chief Justice William Rehnquist*	1972–	Nixon (Rep)	*
*Became Chief Justice in 1986			

similar to their own. In the modern era, the Democratic Party has tended toward liberal political positions, which favor individual rights and government action to bring about social change. The Republican Party embodies conservative views, favoring established institutions and a hands-off approach to social change. In general, courts dominated by Democratic presidential appointees have tended toward more liberal interpretations of law and the Constitution, while those dominated by Republican appointees have taken a more conservative approach.

The nine justices in the *Bakke* case represented a wide range of political and legal views. Far from arriving at a unanimous decision on the case, they produced six separate opinions. Not one of these opinions, however, could be called an opinion of the Court, because not one of them was signed by a majority of five justices. The *Bakke* decision, in short, was about as split as a decision could be.

Use of Race Permitted	UCDMS Program Unlawful but Use of Race Permitted	Admit Bakke	Wrote Opinion
		*	
*			*
		*	
*			*
*			*
*			*
	*	*	*
		*	*
		*	

When the wives of several justices arrived and took seats in the gallery, the observers knew that an important decision was at hand. Today must be the day that *Bakke* would be resolved.

Using a traditional term for opening a law session, the marshal of the court called out, "Oyez! Oyez! Oyez! The Court is now sitting." After a few minor pieces of business, Powell spoke into his microphone. He began by pointing out the immense amount of media attention and public interest in the *Bakke* case. He remarked that the Court spoke on the case with "a notable lack of unanimity." Then he answered the question that everyone was asking.

WHO WON?

The Court's decision, Powell explained in a few short sentences, was that Bakke must be admitted to the University of California at Davis Medical School—and also that the school *could* use race as a consideration in admitting students. On the first point, the Court had upheld the California Supreme Court's decision. On the second, it had reversed it.

"The Decision Everybody Won" is how the *Wall Street Journal* headlined the *Bakke* announcement. The *Los Angeles Times* ran two headlines side by side, reflecting two ways of looking at the split decision. One said, "Historic Ruling Strikes Down Davis Quotas." The other: "School Ruling Seen as a Victory for Civil Rights."

In a nutshell, the Supreme Court ruled that race could be one factor among other factors in admissions decisions, as long as no quotas were set. But it would have taken a forest's worth of nutshells to contain the full text of the opinions delivered by the Court in *Bakke*. Six justices had written separate opinions that totalled 154 pages in the *U.S. Supreme Court Reports*. It took more than an hour for Powell and the other authors to read highlights from their opinions and explain their reasoning.

Powell was the author of the plurality opinion because he agreed in part with each of the "gangs of four" that had lined up on opposite sides of the case. Justice John Paul Stevens wrote a separate opinion for the four who considered the UCDMS plan illegal and wanted to uphold all of the California Supreme Court's decision. Burger, Potter Stewart, and William Rehnquist were the other members of that group. Justice William Brennan wrote a separate opinion for the four who wanted to reverse the California decision and supported the UCDMS program completely, on both statutory and constitutional grounds. The other three in this group were Byron White, Blackmun, and Thurgood Marshall. Each of these three also wrote an individual opinion.

White's opinion dealt with a technical point of law: whether a private person could sue under Title VI of the Civil Rights Act. Blackmun's opinion said that although a race-neutral or color-blind affirmative action program was the ideal, it was currently impossible. He hoped that in the future, affirmative action programs would be a relic of the past, no longer needed. But, said Blackmun, "we must first take account of race. . . . And in order to treat some persons equally, we must treat them differently. We cannot—we dare not—let the Equal Protection Clause perpetuate racial supremacy."

JUSTICE THURGOOD MARSHALL, WHO HAD SERVED ON THE LEGAL STAFF OF THE
NATIONAL ASSOCIATION FOR THE ADVANCEMENT OF COLORED PEOPLE (NAACP)
BEFORE BEING APPOINTED TO THE SUPREME COURT, FOUGHT LONG AND TIRE-
LESSLY FOR CIVIL RIGHTS ON BOTH SIDES OF THE JUDICIAL BENCH.

Marshall's opinion opened with a powerful image: "Three hundred and fifty years ago, the Negro was dragged to this country in chains to be sold into slavery. Uprooted from his homeland and thrust into bondage for forced labor, the slave was deprived of all legal rights." Marshall reminded listeners of the legally enforced enslavement and discrimination that blacks had endured in the nation's history—an experience unlike that of any other group in the population. "Measured by any benchmark of comfort or achievement, meaningful equality remains a distant dream for the Negro," Marshall declared. He concluded by pointing out an ironic fact: blacks had been discriminated against as a group for several hundred years, but now the Court refused to allow a remedy that was based on membership in a group.

SIX
AFFIRMATIVE ACTION
AFTER *BAKKE*

WHAT EFFECT DID THE Supreme Court's *Bakke*
decision have? For one thing, it got Allan Bakke into
medical school.

Throughout the lawsuit Allan Bakke had steadfastly
refused to become a public figure or a spokesman for a
cause. He continued to work as an aerospace engineer and
protected his privacy. On the historic day when the U.S.
Supreme Court delivered its opinion in his case, Bakke
wasn't in the courtroom. He was home in California, with
reporters camped out in front of his house. California time
is three hours behind Washington, D.C., time, which
meant that Bakke received word of the Court's ruling in
the morning. He hurried out of his house, shielding his
face from photographers by holding up a newspaper, and
got in his car and drove to work as he did every day.
Through his attorney, Reynold Colvin, Bakke released a
brief statement: "I am pleased and, after five years of waiting, I look forward to entering medical school in the fall."

Bakke did enter UCDMS in September 1978. As the
thirty-eight-year-old student walked to his first classes,
he passed a group of about a hundred protestors who were
chanting, "Smash the *Bakke* decision now!" He ignored
them, and they appeared not to notice him. For the most
part, Bakke's classmates took a cautious stance. Several

ALLAN BAKKE IS TRAILED BY NEWS AND TELEVISION REPORTERS AFTER ATTENDING HIS FIRST DAY AT THE UNIVERSITY OF CALIFORNIA AT DAVIS MEDICAL SCHOOL ON SEPTEMBER 25, 1978. THE U.S. SUPREME COURT ORDERED THE UNIVERSITY TO ADMIT HIM.

minority medical students told reporters that they had no plans to make Bakke personally uncomfortable, even though some thought he had dealt a crippling blow to civil rights. One second-year student, Sharon Jackson, said, "If it took 200 years to build a house and someone comes along with a match and tries to burn it down, how would you feel? We don't want the house burned down!" Four years later, Bakke quietly graduated from medical school and moved on to a physician's internship at the Mayo Clinic in his birth state of Minnesota. By that time, the California Superior Court had ordered the University of California to pay $183,089 toward the cost of Colvin's legal services.

As part of the ongoing ebb and flow of American race relations, the *Bakke* case became a symbol. To some, it signalled an alarming retreat from the national commitment to civil rights and racial equality. They saw *Bakke* as part of a growing trend: a backlash against affirmative action. The Reverend Jesse Jackson, a nationally known African-American civil rights leader, expressed this view when he called the *Bakke* decision part of a "move to the right"—in other words, in a conservative direction. Student groups that had organized to support UCDMS's policy took an even grimmer tone, calling the Court's opinion "a bad decision with potentially devastating impact on race relations in this country."

Others thought that the *Bakke* decision had not gone far enough. They wanted to see race banned entirely from admissions—and from other choices in public life as well. Conservative law professor Robert H. Bork represented this view, and in the 1980s President

IN JULY 1987, PRESIDENT RONALD REAGAN (RIGHT) INTRODUCED ROBERT BORK (LEFT) AS HIS NOMINEE TO FILL THE SUPREME COURT SEAT OF JUSTICE LEWIS F. POWELL, WHO WAS RETIRING FROM THE COURT; CONGRESS, HOWEVER, DID NOT CONFIRM THE NOMINATION. BORK, LIKE REAGAN, WAS FIRMLY OPPOSED TO ALL FORMS OF AFFIRMATIVE ACTION.

Ronald Reagan, who wanted to end all forms of affirmative action, shared it. (Reagan tried to have Bork appointed to the Supreme Court, but Congress did not approve the nomination.) Many Americans, though, fell somewhere in the middle. They agreed with the Court that although quotas were wrong, affirmative action could be appropriate— if carefully defined and correctly applied. This middle-of-the-road view was summed up in the 1990s by President Bill Clinton's position on affirmative action: "Mend it, don't end it."

Although the great majority of black, Hispanic, and civil rights organizations

PRESIDENT GEORGE W. BUSH LOOKS ON AS LINDA CHAVEZ ADDRESSES THE PRESS IN EARLY 2001. BUSH, A CONSERVATIVE REPUBLICAN, HAD BEEN ELECTED PRESIDENT AND HAD NAMED CHAVEZ TO THE POST OF SECRETARY OF LABOR.

have continued to support affirmative action, some African Americans and members of other minority groups disagree. Linda Chavez, a Hispanic columnist who has served as staff director of the U.S. Commission on Civil Rights and as a member of the United Nations Human Rights Commission, heads an anti-affirmative action organization called the Center for Equal Opportunity, which "supports colorblind public policies and seeks to block the expansion of racial preferences and to prevent their use in employment, education, and voting." Chavez believes that racial preferences are unfair. In addition,

CLARENCE THOMAS REPLACED THURGOOD MARSHALL ON THE SUPREME COURT IN 1991. UNLIKE MARSHALL, THOMAS IS CRITICAL OF AFFIRMATIVE ACTION AND CONSERVATIVE IN HIS VIEWS.

she feels that affirmative action works to lower expectations for minorities, as though saying that minority
individuals cannot succeed on their own merits, without
special help. That view is shared by Clarence Thomas, an
African American who is now a justice on the U.S.
Supreme Court. Thomas has spoken of "adverse stigmatic
effects," or psychological harm, to people who benefit
from affirmative action programs, because those people
and others may feel that their achievements are due to the
programs, not to their abilities.

With such a wide range of opinions about affirmative
action, it's no surprise that ever since *Bakke*, the issue has
continued to evolve. Important twists and turns in the
story of affirmative action have taken place in the nation's
voting booths, legislatures, courtrooms, and universities.

PUTTING IT TO THE VOTE

One of the strongest critics of affirmative action has been
an African-American businessman named Ward Connerly,
who is firmly opposed to what he considers reverse
discrimination. In the mid–1990s, he led the California
Civil Rights Initiative, a movement to get Californians to
vote down affirmative action in their state.

By that time, affirmative action had become a hot
political issue. Democratic President Clinton was
struggling to defend the principle and policies of affirmative action, which came under increasing attack as
conservative Republicans gained power in Congress.
Even some Republicans who had formerly supported
affirmative action were now backing away from the
issue. One of them was Bob Dole, a senator and presidential candidate, who said in 1995, "After nearly thirty
years of government-sanctioned quotas, time tables,

set-asides, and other racial preferences, the American people sense all too clearly that the race-counting game has gone too far."

Connerly led a statewide drive to place a measure called Proposition 209 on the California ballot in 1996. The measure called for an end to all preferences based on "race, sex, color, ethnicity, or national origin in the operation of public employment, education, or public contracting." Supported by California's Republican governor, the measure passed with the approval of more than 54 percent of voters. Civil rights groups tried to block it. They took their case against 209 all the way to the U.S. Supreme Court, which refused to grant certiorari. The result: Proposition 209 became law.

Connerly expanded his organization into the American Civil Rights Institute (ACRI), dedicated to passing similar laws in other states. In 1998, Connerly's group and other activists got Initiative 200, which used the same wording as Proposition 209, placed on the ballot in Washington State. *The New York Times* called the Pacific Northwest state "ground zero in the nation's ongoing war over affirmative action." The Washington initiative, like the California proposition, was passed by the voters—with 58 percent in favor—and became law. ACRI and other conservative groups have tried to organize support for similar measures in other states; so far, none have passed.

LEGAL LANDMARKS

When the *Bakke* case came to the U.S. Supreme Court, interested parties on both sides of the issue knew that the Court's decision would become a precedent that other courts would follow in judging affirmative action cases. They hoped that the *Bakke* decision would be clear and straightforward, offering unmistakable guidelines for future action. What they got was a cluster of differing—sometimes conflicting—views. Justice Lewis F. Powell's plurality opinion, which tried to balance support for some kind of affirmative action with a ruling against the use of quotas, became the precedent. Since 1978, courts at all levels have taken it into consideration when making decisions about affirmative action.

Several key cases have shaped affirmative action law since *Bakke*. The 1979 case of *United Steelworkers of America* v. *Weber* involved the Kaiser Aluminum plant in Gramercy, Louisiana. The local community was about 40 percent black, but fewer than 2 percent of the plant's skilled craft workers were African Americans. To correct this imbalance, plant managers and the workers' union (USWA) agreed on an affirmative action plan. Until the racial mix of skilled workers in the plant matched that of the community, at least half of all employees admitted to the craft training program would be black. Brian Weber, a white employee who hadn't been admitted to the training program, sued the USWA. The case rose to the U.S. Supreme Court, which ruled that private employers could voluntarily adopt affirmative action plans. Some observers, however, felt that the lawsuit may actually have discouraged affirmative action by making labor unions less willing to support plans like Kaiser's.

In the 1980 case of *Fullilove* v. *Klutznick*, the U.S. Supreme Court upheld a portion of the Public Works Employment Act of 1977 that set aside 10 percent of government construction contracts for minority-owned contractors and other small businesses. Before the act, almost no minority businesses had ever received government building contracts. The Court ruled that in passing the law, the U.S. Congress had been trying to correct a large and longstanding inequality.

The 1986 case of *Wygant* v. *Board of Education* involved a complaint by white schoolteachers who were laid off from their jobs. Minority teachers with less seniority had kept their jobs, however, because the school district and the teacher's union had agreed that layoffs would be carried out according to racial percentages in the workforce, not according to seniority. The case was heard by a U.S. Supreme Court that was shifting toward a more conservative approach to affirmative action. Only one justice had changed since *Bakke*: Sandra Day O'Connor, the Court's first woman justice, had replaced Potter Stewart. But the liberal views of Thurgood Marshall, William Brennan, and Harry A. Blackmun, who had evaluated the concept of "equal protection" in light of history and social context, were outweighed by the Court's growing focus on narrower, stricter interpretation of laws, including the Fourteenth Amendment. As a whole, the Court was less willing to see short-term racial preference as a corrective to longstanding past prejudice. Instead, it looked at the law as truly color-blind. The Court found that the agreement violated the equal protection clause of the Fourteenth Amendment.

In 1995, fifteen years after the *Fullilove* case, the case of *Adarand* v. *Peña* forced the Court to take another look at minority business set-asides. *Adarand* involved a contract to install highway guardrails in Colorado's San Juan National Forest. Adarand Constructors, the contracting firm that turned in the lowest bid for the job, was owned by a white man. Mountain Gravel, the company doing the hiring, was working under a federal contract from the Department of Transportation, which had minority business set-asides. Mountain Gravel passed over Adarand in favor of a Hispanic-owned contractor. Adarand sued, naming U.S. Secretary of Transportation Federico Peña as respondent, and took the case to the U.S. Supreme Court.

Significant changes had occurred in the composition of the Supreme Court—and in its viewpoints—since the *Wygant* decision of 1986. Already leaning in a conservative direction at the time of *Wygant*, the Court had become more conservative with the appointments of new justices by Republican presidents Ronald Reagan and George H. W. Bush. Reagan, who had appointed Sandra Day O'Connor to the Court, nominated Antonin Scalia in 1986, when Chief Justice Warren E. Burger retired. William H. Rehnquist became the new chief justice, and Scalia replaced Rehnquist as an associate justice. Reagan's final appointee was Anthony M. Kennedy. In 1988 Kennedy replaced Powell, the justice who had cast the key swing vote in the *Bakke* case.

Reagan was followed by another Republican president, the first George Bush. Like Reagan, Bush nominated Supreme Court justices who shared his conservative views. The first was David Souter, who replaced Brennan in 1990. The following year, Marshall retired, and Bush replaced him with Clarence Thomas. Like Marshall, Thomas was African American, but his views were far more conservative than those of his predecessor in the Court. For example, Thomas strongly opposed affirmative action, the cause for which Marshall had argued vigorously in *Bakke*.

The Democrats returned to the White House under President William J. Clinton in 1992, who made two appointments to the Court. Ruth Bader Ginsburg, the

Court's second woman justice, replaced White in 1993. The next year, Stephen G. Breyer replaced Blackmun. Although Clinton's appointees held more liberal views than the justices chosen by the previous Republican presidents, their influence on the Court was outweighed by the larger bloc of conservative justices. This meant that when *Adarand* came before the Court in 1995, it faced a much more conservative group than earlier affirmative action cases had encountered.

The *Adarand* case became extremely complex. In her 2002 book *Affirmative Action*, Rachel Krantz notes that it "has gone to the Supreme Court three times, with three different names, through three presidential administrations, and a great many changes in the affirmative action policy that was originally challenged." As a result of the changes in the composition of the Supreme Court, the outcome of *Adarand* was quite different from that of *Fullilove*, the earlier case involving minority business set-asides. Where *Fullilove* had broadly supported the use of set-asides in federal contracting, *Adarand* strictly limited it. Two of the justices in *Adarand*, Scalia and Thomas, wanted to ban all forms of affirmative action completely. Thomas wrote: "Government-sponsored racial discrimination based on benign prejudice is just as noxious as discrimination inspired by malicious prejudice. In each instance, it is racial discrimination, plain and simple." A five-justice majority, however, agreed that the lingering effects of racial discrimination made race-based remedies allowable in certain very closely defined circumstances. The bottom line of the Court's *Adarand* decision was that public programs could still give preference to minorities, but only under specific, limited conditions. In the words of Justice O'Connor, who wrote the majority opinion for the Court:

> All racial classifications, imposed by whatever fed-
> eral, state, or local governmental actor, must be
> analyzed by a reviewing court under strict scrutiny.
> In other words, such classifications are constitu-
> tional only if they are narrowly tailored measures
> that further compelling governmental interests.

To meet strict scrutiny standards, programs showing racial classification or preference would have to be tem-porary, designed to correct actual discrimination suffered by individuals in the past, and focused on specific results. *Adarand* did not end affirmative action programs, but it drastically limited their scope. Another result of the Court's conservative ruling in *Adarand* was that it encour-aged those who opposed affirmative action in education to keep questioning the *Bakke* decision and challenging it in the courts.

classrooms and courtrooms

The *Bakke* case dealt with affirmative action in higher education. Since the case, the campuses of the nation's colleges and universities have seen a number of important developments in affirmative action policy and law. Some of them concerned the University of California, where the *Bakke* case was born.

The effects of affirmative action rulings are hard to measure. Statistics such as minority enrollments can't be clearly tied to a particular court decision, policy change, or law. Still, trends in such statistics reflect the general climate of affirmative action. In a 1999 book called

The Shape of the River: Long Term Consequences of Considering Race in College and University Admissions, William G. Bowen and Derek Bok, former presidents of Princeton University and Harvard University respectively, analyzed the surveys of more than 60,000 students. They concluded that Justice Powell's opinion in *Bakke* played a crucial role in encouraging very selective colleges and professional schools to continue considering race in admitting students. These decisions, Bowen and Bok argue, contributed to the growth of a black middle class in the United States. They also improved race relations among both white and minority students by promoting campus integration.

But affirmative action has run into problems in institutions of higher learning. In the mid–1990s, Ward Connerly—one of the chief sponsors of the anti-affirmative action Proposition 209—was also one of the regents of the University of California, the same body that had defended UCDMS's special admissions program two decades earlier. By this time the regents had come to oppose affirmative action, and Connerly led them in a vote to end all consideration of race in admissions to professional and graduate programs, without waiting for 209 to become law. The new policy went into effect in 1996. The following year, enrollment of African Americans in the law school of the University of California at Berkeley dropped by 81 percent, from seventy-five to fourteen students. Overall admission of black, Hispanic, and Native American students to Berkeley fell by half. For the 1998–1999 year, only 98 of the 3,600 new students were African American.

But while minority admissions fell at Berkeley and the University of California at Los Angeles, considered the most prestigious campuses in the UC system, they rose at some of the other campuses in the system.

University administrators started to worry that UC would turn into a two-tier system, with minorities confined to certain campuses. In the spring of 1999, the university adopted a new admissions policy under which the top 4 percent of high-school students in the state are guaranteed admission to any UC campus. Similar programs are now in place in other state university systems. Texas's Top Ten program, for instance, guarantees the top 10 percent of the state's high-school seniors admission to the campus of their choice.

The *DeFunis* and *Bakke* cases had questioned the legality of prefential admissions in professional schools. The 1996 case of *Hopwood* v. *Texas* once again raised the troubling issue of reverse discrimination in a professional school. Cheryl Hopwood and other white students who had been rejected by the University of Texas law school sued the school, claiming their Fourteenth Amendment right to equal protection under the law had been violated because the law school had an affirmative action policy. The students wanted the policy stopped. They also wanted monetary compensation for the lifetime loss of earnings they claimed to have suffered by not being able to attend the school. The school, in turn, argued that Hopwood and the others would not have been admitted even without an affirmative action policy, and that the state had a compelling interest in furthering desegregation, correcting past discrimination, and promoting diversity. The case never reached the U.S. Supreme Court, which refused to grant certiorari, but the lower court ruled that the school's use of race was unconstitutional. Although Hopwood and the other students received only token amounts of money beyond their court costs, the decision effectively ended affirmative action in Texas.

Reverse discrimination, it seems, is a claim that will

MARY SUE COLEMAN, PRESIDENT OF THE UNIVERSITY OF MICHIGAN, APPEARED BEFORE THE U.S. SUPREME COURT BUILDING IN 2003, WHEN THE COURT, IN A SPLIT DECISION, FOUND THE UNIVERSITY'S UNDERGRADUATE ADMISSIONS POLICY UNCONSTITUTIONAL BUT SUPPORTED THAT OF ITS LAW SCHOOL.

not go away. In the spring of 2003, the U.S. Supreme Court delivered decisions in two cases, both of which involved the University of Michigan in Ann Arbor. They were the Court's first rulings on affirmative action in higher education since *Bakke*, twenty-five years earlier. "Many civil rights lawyers," *Time* magazine declared as the case neared its conclusion, "agree that the University of Michigan could be the Alamo of affirmative action, the place where they make their last stand."

Both cases named Lee Bollinger, an official of the university at the time. *Gratz* v. *Bollinger* concerned a high-school senior, Jennifer Gratz, whose application had been rejected even though some minority students with lower grades and test scores had been admitted. The university used a "point" system in which African-American, Hispanic, and Native American applicants received extra points on their applications (so did athletes, economically disadvantaged students, and students from mostly minority high schools). *Grutter* v. *Bollinger* was the case of Barbara Grutter, a white woman in her forties who applied to the university's law school and was rejected. She sued on the same grounds Bakke had used. Both women received free legal services from the Center for Individual Rights, a nonprofit law group that had also represented Hopwood. The Supreme Court chose to hear and decide on the cases at the same time.

Many individuals and groups filed amicus briefs supporting one side or the other of the Michigan cases. Among those who sided with Gratz and Grutter were President Bush's administration; the state of Florida and Florida Governor Jeb Bush, brother of the president;

STUDENTS FROM THE UNIVERSITY OF MICHIGAN STAND BEFORE THE
U.S. SUPREME COURT BUILDING IN WASHINGTON TO PROTEST RACE-BASED
ADMISSIONS POLICIES. IN A CASE INVOLVING THE UNIVERSITY'S LAW SCHOOL,
THE COURT UPHELD THE USE OF RACE AS ONE FACTOR IN ADMISSIONS.

the Asian American Legal Foundation; Connerly; and a
number of conservative organizations. Among those
who took the other side, supporting the university's affirmative action programs, were the American Jewish
Committee; the General Motors Corporation and a
number of other large businesses; Harvard, Howard,
Stanford, and many other universities; the National
Education Association; and the National Urban League,

a longtime supporter of African-American advancement.

Like *Bakke*, the two Michigan cases produced a split result. In each case, four of the justices took a conservative position and four a more liberal stance. The deciding vote in each case was that of Justice O'Connor, who sided with the conservatives in one case and with the liberals in the other.

In *Gratz*, the conservative bloc was led by Chief Justice Rehnquist, who was supported by Justices Scalia, Kennedy, Thomas, and O'Connor. By a five to four majority, the Court declared the University of Michigan's undergraduate admissions system unconstitutional. The justices ruled that although achieving diversity is a compelling state interest that allows race to be used among other factors in university admissions, the university's program failed to meet the necessary strict scrutiny standards. The program, which automatically favored minorities with a set number of points in the admissions process, was not narrowly tailored to achieve a limited, specific result.

In *Grutter*, the Court supported the law school's admissions policy by a five to four majority. O'Connor sided with Justices Stevens, Breyer, Ginsburg, and Souter in finding that the law school's admissions decisions were based on individual review and did not employ quotas, points, or set figures. It also ruled that the state's compelling interest in diversity still held. In the end, *Grutter* reaffirmed the basic ruling in *Bakke*. If the University of Michigan *was* affirmative action's Alamo, it didn't end like the original Alamo, with a massacre.

SANDRA DAY O'CONNOR, THE FIRST WOMAN TO BECOME A SUPREME COURT JUSTICE, CAST THE DECIDING SWING VOTES IN THE *GRATZ* AND *GRUTTER* AFFIRMATIVE ACTION CASES, AS LEWIS F. POWELL HAD DONE IN *BAKKE*.

Affirmative action is now more controversial, and more complicated, than it was in the late 1960s and the 1970s, in the heyday and the aftermath of the civil rights movement. The message that *Bakke* sent to school administrators and admissions committees was, "You can use affirmative action, but with care." Still, many educational and professional leaders remain committed to affirmative action as a vital step toward diversity in the country's schools and professions. In November of 1999, for example, Gregory Williams, president of the Association of American Law Schools, wrote in the group's newsletter, "While I urge us not to lose sight of the fact that *Bakke* is still good law, we cannot totally rely on legal cases to support our diversity efforts. . . . We need to think about ways we can carry our message of the value and importance of diversity to the public."

Perhaps people on both sides of the affirmative action issue would agree with O'Connor, who wrote in the *Grutter* opinion, "We expect that 25 years from now, the use of racial preferences will no longer be necessary to further the interest approved today." Like Justice Blackmun when he wrote his opinion in *Bakke* twenty-five years before, O'Connor looked forward to a time when affirmative action will no longer be necessary because integration and equality will have become reality.

TImeLIne

1896
U.S. Supreme Court rules "separate but equal" accommodations for blacks and whites constitutional in *Plessy* v. *Ferguson*

1954
In *Brown* v. *Board of Education*, the Supreme Court finds racially segregated education unconstitutional

1961
President John F. Kennedy's Executive Order 10925 creates Equal Employment Opportunity Commission (EEOC) and instructs federal contractors to take "affirmative action" to avoid discrimination

1964
Civil Rights Act of 1964 bans discrimination based on race, color, religion, or national origin in a wide range of circumstances

1967
President Lyndon B. Johnson's Executive Order 11246 strengthens affirmative action policies for government contractors

1970
Medical School of the University of California at Davis (UCDMS) begins affirmative action to increase student diversity

1973
Allan Bakke, who is white, is denied admission to UCDMS for 1973–1974 year

April 1974
Supreme Court dismisses *DeFunis* v. *Odegaard*, the case of a white student who claimed to have been unfairly denied admission to law school; Bakke is again rejected by UCDMS, this time for 1974–1975 year

June 1974
Bakke sues University of California Regents in California Superior Court

November 1974
Superior Court orders UCDMS to end affirmative action admissions but does not order it to admit Bakke

May 1975
University of California Regents appeal superior court decision to California Supreme Court

September 1976
California Supreme Court upholds superior court decision and orders UCDMS to admit Bakke

December 1976
Regents of the University of California appeal California Supreme Court decision to U.S. Supreme Court

February 22, 1977
Supreme Court agrees to hear *Bakke* case the following October

October 1977
Fifty-eight amicus curiae briefs have been filed in connection with *Bakke*

October 12, 1977
Court hears oral arguments in *Bakke*

October 14, 1977
Court holds first closed conference to discuss *Bakke*

October 17, 1977
Court requests additional briefs on Title VI of Civil Rights Act

May 1, 1978
Justice Harry Blackmun casts final vote in *Bakke*

June 28, 1978
Supreme Court rules against UCDMS's fixed-quota admissions program, orders UCDMS to admit Bakke, and allows schools to consider race among other factors in admissions

September 1978
Bakke enters UCDMS

1982
Bakke graduates from UCDMS

1995

In *Adarand* v. *Peña*, Supreme Court rules that public programs using racial set-asides must meet strict scrutiny standards

1996

In *Hopwood* v. *Texas*, U.S. Fifth Circuit Court of Appeals rules that Texas schools cannot use race in admissions; Proposition 209 becomes law in California, banning affirmative action in public schools, agencies, and contractors

1998

Initiative 200, similar to Proposition 209, becomes law in Washington State

2003

In reverse-discrimination cases *Gratz* v. *Bollinger* and *Grutter* v. *Bollinger*, Supreme Court bans quota-like undergraduate admissions policies but allows the use of race among other factors to achieve diversity

NOTES

Chapter 1

p. 8, Allan P. Sindler. *Bakke, DeFunis, and Minority Admissions*. New York and London: Longman, 1978, p. 254.

p. 8, Howard Ball. *The Bakke Case: Race, Education, and Affirmative Action*. Lawrence: University Press of Kansas, 2000, p. 88.

p. 9, Sindler, p. 72.

p. 11, Joel Dreyfuss and Charles Lawrence III. *The Bakke Case: The Politics of Inequality*. New York: Harcourt Brace Jovanovich, 1979, p. 28

p. 13, Sindler, p. 65.

p. 13, Dreyfuss and Lawrence, p. 16.

p. 14, Sindler, p. 67.

p. 17, Dreyfuss and Lawrence, p. 14.

p. 17, Sindler. pp. 70, 71.

p. 19, Farmer-Rodino Hearings before Subcommittee No. 5 of the Committee on the Judiciary, House of Representatives, 88th Congress, 2238–41, July 26, 1963, quoted in Terry H. Anderson. *The Pursuit of Fairness: A History of Affirmative Action*. New York: Oxford University Press, 2004, p. 283.

p. 20, U.S. Census Bureau. "Population by Race and Hispanic or Latino Origin for the United States, Regions, Divisions, States, Puerto Rico, and Places of 100,000 or More Population," April 21, 2001. http://www.census.gov/population/cen2000/phc–t6/tab02.pdf

p. 20, Frank Hobbs and Nicole Stoops. "Demographic Trends in the 20th Century," U.S. Census Bureau, November, 2002. http://www.cen-sus.gov/prod/2002pubs/censr–4.pdf

pp. 20–21, U.S. Census Bureau. "U.S. Interim Projections by Age, Sex, Race, and Hispanic Origin," March 18, 2004. http://www.census.gov/ipc/www/usin-terimproj/

p. 21, Quoted in Terry Anderson. *The Pursuit of Fairness: A History of Affirmative Action*. New York: Oxford University Press, 2004,

Chapter 2

p. 22, Philip F. Rubio. *A History of Affirmative Action: 1619–2000*. Jackson: University Press of Mississippi, 2001, p. 4.

p. 25, Rubio, p. 11.

p. 28, *University of California Regents v. Bakke*, 428 U.S. 265 (1978).

p. 28, Rachel Krantz. *Affirmative Action*. New York: Facts On File, 2002.

p. 30, Terry Anderson. *The Pursuit of Fairness: A History of Affirmative Action*. New York: Oxford University Press, 2004, pp. 2–3.

p. 31, *Plessy v. Ferguson*, 163 U.S. 537 (1896).

p. 32, Anderson, p.6.

p. 34, *Brown v. Board of Education*, 347 U.S. 483 (1954).

p. 37, Krantz, p. 32.

p. 38, Howard Ball. *The Bakke Case: Race, Education, and Affirmative Action*. Lawrence: University Press of Kansas, p. 8.

p. 38, Krantz, p. 33.

p. 39, Krantz, p. 16.

p. 40, Joel Dreyfuss and Charles Lawrence III. *The Bakke Case: The Politics of Inequality*. New York: Harcourt Brace Jovanovich, 1979, p. 7.

Chapter 3

p. 43, Allan P. Sindler. *Bakke, DeFunis, and Minority Admissions*. New York and London: Longman, 1978, p. 29.

p. 43, Sindler, p. 29.

p. 44, Sindler, p. 38.

p. 44, Sindler, p. 34.

p. 45, Howard Ball. *The Bakke Case: Race, Education, and Affirmative Action*. Lawrence: University Press of Kansas, 2000, p. 23.

p. 47, Ball pp. 24-25 and Sindler, pp.34–38.

p. 49, Sindler, p. 194.

p.50, Ball, p. 28.

p. 52, http://www.supremecourtus.gov/about/justicecaselaod.pdf

p. 56, *DeFunis v. Odegaard*, 416 U.S. 312 (1974).

p. 57, *DeFunis v. Odegaard*, 416 U.S. 312 (1974).

p. 58, Ball, p. 31.

p. 58, *DeFunis v. Odegaard*, 416 U.S. 312 (1974).

p. 60, *DeFunis v. Odegaard*, 416 U.S. 312 (1974).

p. 61, *DeFunis v. Odegaard*, 416 U.S. 312 (1974).

p. 61, Ball, pp. 27–28.

p. 66, Ball, p. 44.

Chapter 4

p. 68, *University of California Regents v. Bakke*, 438 U.S. 265 (1978). Joel Dreyfuss and Charles Lawrence III. *The Bakke Case: The Politics of Inequality*. New York: Harcourt Brace Jovanovich, 1979, p. 27.

p. 68, Howard Ball. *The Bakke Case: Race, Education, and Affirmative Action*. Lawrence: University Press of Kansas, p. 55.

p. 70, "UC Official Suggested Bakke Suit," *San Francisco Sunday Examiner and Chronicle*, February 13, 1977. Quoted in Allan P. Sindler. *Bakke, DeFunis, and Minority Admissions*. New York and London: Longman, 1978, p. 70.

p. 70, Letters to the editor, *The New York Times*. July 3, 1977. Quoted in Sindler, p. 70.

p. 70, "UC Official Suggested Bakke Suit," *San Francisco Sunday Examiner and Chronicle*. February 13, 1977. Quoted in Sindler, p. 70.

p. 71, Dreyfuss and Lawrence, pp. 21–22.

p. 71, Dreyfuss and Lawrence, p. 22.

p. 72, Dreyfuss and Lawrence, p. 26.

p. 73, "UC Official Suggested Bakke Suit," *San Francisco Sunday Examiner and Chronicle*. February 13, 1977. Quoted in Sindler, p. 73.

p. 73, pp. 22–23.

p. 73, Dreyfuss and Lawrence, pp. 28–29.

p. 75, Dreyfuss and Lawrence, p. 29.

p. 75, Dreyfuss and Lawrence, p. 34.

p. 78, Ball, p. 57.

p. 78, Dreyfuss and Lawrence, p. 64.

p. 79, Dreyfuss and Lawrence, p. 69.

p. 80, Dreyfuss and Lawrence, p. 69.

p. 81, Dreyfuss and Lawrence, p. 73.

p. 82, Ball, pp. 60–61.

p. 85, Ball, p. 65.

Chapter 5

p. 87, Howard Ball. *The Bakke Case: Race, Education, and Affirmative Action*. Lawrence: University Press of Kansas, 2000, p. 1.

p. 87, *University of California Regents* v. *Bakke*, 438 U.S. 265 (1978).

p. 87, Quoted in Ball, p. 77.

p. 89, *University of California Regents* v. *Bakke*.

p. 89, *University of California Regents* v. *Bakke*.

p. 89, Joel Dreyfuss and Charles Lawrence III. *The Bakke Case: The Politics of Inequality*. New York: Harcourt Brace Jovanovich, 1979, p. 170.

p. 90, Ball, p. 80.

p. 93, Ball, p. 176.

p. 93, Ball, p. 176.

pp. 93–94, *San Francisco Chronicle*. June 28, 1978. Quoted in Allan P. Sindler. *Bakke, DeFunis, and Minority Admissions*. New York and London: Longman, 1978, p. 242.

p. 94, *University of California Regents* v. *Bakke*.
pp. 94–95, *University of California Regents* v. *Bakke*.
p. 96, *University of California Regents* v. *Bakke*.
p. 96, Ball, pp. 98, 107, 118–119, 141.
p. 98, Ball, pp. 98, 107, 118–119, 141.
p. 98, Ball, pp. 98, 107, 118–119, 141.
p. 102, Ball, pp. 98, 107, 118–119, 141.
p. 105, *University of California Regents* v. *Bakke*.
p. 105, *University of California Regents* v. *Bakke*.

Chapter 6
p. 106, Joel Dreyfuss and Charles Lawrence III. *The Bakke Case: The Politics of Inequality*. New York: Harcourt Brace Jovanovich, 1979, pp. 225–226, and p. 143, and Howard Ball, *The Bakke Case: Race, Education, and Affirmative Action*. Lawrence: University Press of Kansas, 2000.
p. 107, Ball, pp. 173 and 143.
p. 108, Dreyfuss and Lawrence, pp. 226–227.
p. 109, http://www.lindachavez.org
p. 111, Ball, pp. 183–184.
p. 112, Terry H. Anderson. *The Pursuit of Fairness: A History of Affirmative Action*. New York: Oxford University Press, 2004, p. 235.
p. 112, http://www.acri.org
p. 112, Ball, p. 167.
p. 116, Rachel Krantz. *Affirmative Action*. New York: Facts OnFile, 2002, p. 83.
p. 116, *Adarand Constructors, Inc.* v. *Pena*, 515 U.S. 200 (1995).
p. 117, *Adarand Constructors, Inc.* v. *Pena*, 515 U.S. 200 (1995).
p. 118, Ball, pp. 164 and 167.
p. 121, Anderson, p. 267.
p. 125, Ball, p. 202.
p. 125, *Grutter* v. *Bollinger*, No. 02–241 (2003).

(All Internet sites were accessible as of February 15, 2005.)

Further Information

FURTHER READING
Banfield, Susan. *The Bakke Case: Quotas in College Admissions.* Berkeley Heights, NJ: Enslow Publishers, 1998.

Beckwith, Francis J., and Todd Jones, eds. *Affirmative Action: Social Justice or Reverse Discrimination?* Amherst, NY: Prometheus Books, 1997.

Dudley, William, and Charles Cozie. *Racism in America: Opposing Viewpoints.* San Diego, CA: Greenhaven Press, 1991.

Gold, Susan Dudley. *Brown v. Board of Education: Separate but Equal?* New York: Marshall Cavendish Benchmark, 2005.

Grapes, Bryan J. D. *Affirmative Action.* Farmington Hills, MI: Gale Group, 2000.

Hanmer, Trudy J. *Affirmative Action: Opportunity for All?* Hillside, NJ: Enslow Publishers, 1993.

Krantz, Rachel. *Affirmative Action.* New York: Facts On File, 2002.

LeVert, Suzanne. *The Supreme Court.* New York: Benchmark Books, 2002.

Patrick, John Jay. *The Supreme Court of the United States: A Student Companion.* New York: Oxford University Press Children's Books, 2002.

Urofsky, Melvin I. *A Conflict of Rights: The Supreme Court and Affirmative Action.* New York: Scribner's Sons, 1991.

Woods, Geraldine. *Affirmative Action.* New York: Franklin Watts, 1989.

WEB SITES

Affirmative Action and Diversity Project: A Web Page for Research
http://aad.english.ucsb.edu

American Civil Rights Institute
http://www.acri.org

Americans Against Discrimination and Preferences
http://www.aadap.org

Bakke and Beyond: A History and Timeline of Affirmative Action
http://www.inforplease.com/spot/affirmative1.html

Bakke on FindLaw
http://laws.findlaw.com/us/438/265.html

Landmark Cases: Supreme Court
http://www.landmarkcases.org/bakke/

Legal Information Institute
http://www.law.cornell.edu

TEACHERS' GUIDES

National Association of Criminal Defense Lawyers
www.nacdl.org

Street Law
Provides lesson plans on twenty landmark Supreme Court cases
www.streetlaw.com

BIBLIOGraPHY

BOOKS AND ARTICLES
Anderson, Terry H. *The Pursuit of Fairness: A History of Affirmative Action*. New York: Oxford University Press, 2004.

Ball, Howard. *The Bakke Case: Race, Education, and Affirmative Action*. Lawrence: University Press of Kansas, 2000.

Biskupic, Joan. "Diverse or Discriminatory? Affirmative Action in Education Remains Popular, Despite Setbacks." *USA Today*, October 10, 2001.

Bowen, William C., and Derek Bok. *The Shape of the River: Long Term Consequences of Considering Race in College and University Admissions*. Princeton, NJ: Princeton University Press, 1999.

Chapman, Steven. "Affirmative Action Unhinges a Nation." *Chicago Tribune*, March 31, 1996.

Darity, William, Jr. "Give Affirmative Action Time to Act." *Chronicle of Higher Education*, December 1, 2000.

Dreyfuss, Joel, and Charles Lawrence III. *The Bakke Case and the Politics of Inequality*. New York: Harcourt Brace Jovanovich, 1979.

Eastland, Terry. *Ending Affirmative Action: The Case for Colorblind Justice*. New York: Basic Books, 1996.

Editorial Board. "Bakke's Elegant Compromise." *St. Louis Post-Dispatch*, September 2, 2001.

Gehring, John. "Eyeing Campus Diversity." *Education Week*, 20, No. 43, August 8, 2001.

McCormack, Richard. "Race and the University: Why Social Justice Leads to Academic Excellence." *Seattle Times*, March 19, 2000.

Rubio, Philip F. *A History of Affirmative Action: 1619–2000*. Jackson: University Press of Mississippi, 2001.

Sindler, Allan P. *Bakke, DeFunis, and Minority Admissions*. New York and London: Longman, 1978.

Welch, Susan, and John Gruhl. *Affirmative Action and Minority Enrollments in Medical and Law Schools*. Ann Arbor: University of Michigan Press, 1999.

Wilkinson, J. Harvie. *From Brown to Bakke: The Supreme Court and School Integration, 1954–1978*. New York: Oxford University Press, 1979.

LIST OF CASES AND STATUTES RELATED TO *UNIVERSITY OF CALIFORNIA REGENTS V. BAKKE*

Adarand Constructors, Inc. v. Peña, 515 U.S. 200 (1995) (later *Adarand v. Slater* [2000] and *Adarand v. Mineta* [2001])

Baker v. Carr, 369 U.S. 186 (1962)

Brown v. Board of Education, 347 U.S. 483 (1954)

Civil Rights Act, 1964

Coalition for Economic Equity, et al. v. Pete Wilson, Governor, No. 97-15030, (9th Circuit 1997)

Cooper v. Aaron, 358 U.S. 1 (1958)

DeFunis v. Odegaard, 416 U.S. 312 (1974)

Education Amendments, 1972

Executive Order 11246 (1965), amended by Executive Order 11375 (1967)

Fullilove v. *Klutznick*, 448 U.S. 448 (1980)

Heart of Atlanta Motel v. *United States*, 379 U.S. 241 (1964)

Gratz v. *Bollinger*, No. 02-516 (2003)

Grutter v. *Bollinger*, No. 02-241 (2003)

Hopwood v. *Texas*, 78 F.3d 932, (5th Circuit 1996)

Initiative 200, Washington State, 1998 (Washington State Civil Rights Act)

Johnson v. *Transportation Agency of Santa Clara County*, 480 U.S. 616 (1987)

Korematsu v. *United States*, 323 U.S. 241 (1944)

Loving v. *Virginia*, 388 U.S. 1 (1967)

Metro Broadcasting v. *Federal Communications Commission*, 497 U.S. 547 (1990)

Plessy v. *Ferguson*, 163 U.S. 537 (1896)

Proposition 209, California, 1995 (California Constitution, Amendment to Article I)

Swann v. *Board of Education*, 402 U.S. 1 (1970)

Sweatt v. *Painter*, 339 U.S. 629 (1950)

United States v. *Carolene Products*, 304 U.S. 144 (1938)

United States Constitution Fifth, Thirteenth, Fourteenth, Fifteenth, Nineteenth, and Twenty-Fourth Amendments

United Steelworkers of America v. *Weber*, 443 U.S. 193 (1979)

Webster v. *Reproductive Health Services*, 492 U.S. 490 (1989)

Wygant v. *Board of Education*, 476 U.S. 267 (1986)

index

Page numbers in **boldface** are illustrations, tables, and charts

about the author

REBECCA STEFOFF is the author of many nonfiction books for young adults, including the ten-volume series North American Historical Atlases and the five-volume series World Historical Atlases, both published by Benchmark Books. In addition to books on history, exploration, nature, and science, she has authored works on social history, writing about such topics as environmental activism and legislation, immigration, and Native American rights. Stefoff makes her home in Portland, Oregon. Information about her books for young people can be found at www.rebeccastefoff.com.